'May all beings have happiness and
the causes of happiness.

May all beings be free from suffering
and the causes of suffering.

May all beings never be parted from
freedom's true joy.

May all beings dwell in equanimity,
free from attachment and aversion'.

Buddhist Prayer

THE WAY OF EMOTION

A Path to Liberation

First Edition

Chris T

Divinity
Books

www.divinitybooks.co.uk

Published by Divinity Books,
United Kingdom.
www.divinitybooks.co.uk

The information within this book is for
educational purposes only and is not intended as a substitute
for the medical advice of physicians. The reader should regularly
consult a physician in matters relating to his/her health and
particularly with respect to any symptoms that may require
diagnosis or medical attention.

Please note that this print is an edited version for
under 18/over 12s. For the complete unedited version for
over 18s, see the unedited edition.

THE WAY OF EMOTION

By Chris T

Author's foreword

As we enter the Age of Aquarius, I will reveal to mankind the mysteries of the Soul as they have been revealed to me. Contained within these pages are the ancient mysteries of old pertaining to the science of the Soul but with a modern take on the psycho-spiritual process of awakening.

What I will teach is not new and has been taught for thousands of years throughout various esoteric schools of wisdom and cultures. Some of the best examples of the teachings can be found in religion and the occult schools of wisdom when interpreted in the correct manner in terms of symbols, allegories and parables that relate to psychological, astronomical, physiological and anatomical truths.

This hidden knowledge of every race can be traced back to the legendary mythic figure of Hermes Trismegistus. The hermetic axiom *'As above, so below; As below, so above'* relates to the principle of correspondence and that mankind is always subject to law and phenomena on various planes of existence.

The laws that govern the heavens and planets are the laws that govern you and have universal application. These laws however, can be transcended by those who have done the necessary work to transmute their consciousness into that of the Sun, from lead into gold. Some refer to this process as *'The Great Work'*, *'Alchemy'*, *'Illumination'* or *'Enlightenment'*.

There are many ways to express these truths and I will express them to you as they were expressed to me while on the path of solar initiation. The truth is best experienced as words do not do the transcendent justice however, we will have to do with words until direct experiential knowledge (gnosis) is achieved through the process of a spiritual awakening.

With love,

Chris T

Chapters

References

Introduction

What is Emotion?

E-motion is energy in motion at a particular rate and frequency of vibration. The word *'emotion'* means to go out from, to flow forth. There can be no motion without energy. Energy and spirit can be used to refer to the same thing.

The religious view of emotions being spiritual in nature stands correct as emotions exist as forms of electrical energy that condition the material universe and man likewise. This fact can be verified through illumination and the scientific works of Walter Russell.

Emotions condition us electrically with an ionic charge and research has shown that exposure to high concentrations of positive ions raises the levels of serotonin in the blood, while negative ions have the opposite effect on serotonin levels.

The modern view of emotion as a biological chemical reaction is incorrect as the chemical cascade caused by emotion is an effect of the electrical energies of emotion upon our physical constitution. Emotions and their chemical signatures cause us to think, feel, act and perceive our environment in a very particular way. When we are under the influence of emotion, we are forever moved by the polarised forces within us until enlightenment is achieved.

There are eight basic emotions and one fulcrum which we call rest. These nine altered states of consciousness can be paired into four pairs of opposites and a fulcrum. This division of opposites can then be further divided into positive and negative emotions in the classical sense as follows; -

- Fear & Excitement
- Anger & Desire
- Pain & Love
- Sadness & Happiness

Rest is the still point of potential from which all emotions arise and return to. Rest is the alpha and omega.

In Russellian science, the still point is defined as; -

'The foundation of the spiritual universe is stillness, the balanced stillness of the One magnetic Light of God.

Balanced stillness is the Positive Principle of stability and unity. In it there are no negations.

The foundation of the physical universe is motion; the ever-changing motion arising out of pairs of unbalanced conditions which must forever move to seek the balanced stillness of unity from which they sprang as multiple pairs of units.

Unbalanced motion is the Negative Principle of instability, multiplicity and separateness which is this physical universe of electric octave waves of opposed lights.

In the Negative Principle there is no positive. It is composed entirely of pairs of negations which are forever voiding each other, cancelling each other's action and reaction, thus negating each other by never allowing either one to exceed its fixed zero of universal stillness'.

In Russellian physics what we call motion can be applied to the psychological phenomena of emotion, for it is the same laws that govern both. The motion of energy that conditions the universe externally also conditions us internally and as a result, we think that we are what we feel in terms of emotion.

It is from the mental impressions of the electric sensed universe that we begin to form a mental representation of who we are based on our sensed and societal conditioning. This sense of self and idea of who we are is what is known as the *'Ego'*. The E-go is the false sense of self that commands us into motion. *'E'* denotes energy and *'go'* is the verb conveying action, it is the mode of the mind that is moved by e-motion. Like the sensed universe of motion, the ego is illusory.

What we deem as positive and negative emotions in the classical sense are both negations which result in a sense of separation and incompleteness. The pairs of emotional opposites are of the same whole, but we view and experience them differently as we can only experience one half of the equation at one time.

Each pairing of emotions becomes the invert and reverse of the other. Love, for example, is the positive invert to that of pain, while pain is the negative invert to that of love. Love creates, expands and integrates, while pain destroys, collapses and separates. These opposing forces are of a greater whole that are interconnected and give rise to one another in turn. They are the yin and the yang as described in Chinese philosophy.

Rest is the fulcrum from which all emotions spring. Rest
in psychological terms is referred to as 'Homeostasis',
a steady state of balance and equilibrium.

When stress increases it becomes either fear or excitement,
or anger or desire depending on how we perceive and
appraise the event or situation. The fact that we appraise
these emotions, that is view them subjectively relative to
prior conditioning releases further chemicals in the brain
altering that feeling so in essence the appraisal becomes a
self-fulfilling prophecy. Sensations elicit a chemical reaction
within us which in turn alters our perception of reality and
our perception of reality elicits a chemical reaction within
which in turn alters the sensations that we experience.

Although emotions are energy, because we inhabit
biochemical machines, these emotions elicit specific
chemical reactions within the human body and can be
identified by certain chemical signatures when studying
such phenomena. Emotion and sensation can be subjectively
increased or decreased by altering our chemistry. Pain for
example, whether it be sensed or emotional is a subjective
experience that is regulated by our neurochemistry which
in turn alters our perception of pain. Both types of pain can
be managed using psychoactive substances or by cultural
norms. Some Eastern cultures self-regulate pain via their
appraisal of it without the use of exogenous drugs.

Emotions induce a particular chemistry upon the psyche
which in turn colours our perception and appraisal of a
situation. When we are under the influence of emotion
and its overriding objective, we don't see the world as it
is, we see the world as we are. A deficiency or surplus of
neurochemicals causes us to seek emotional and sensed
pleasures to readdress the internal chemical imbalance

and return to homeostasis.

Emotions cause us to seek sensual pleasures as a means of self-medicating. On a chemical level we seek that which we are lacking while on the energetic or soul level we seek unity with that which we have expelled through the act of sex.

When we polarise the soul, we bring into being polarised emotion. We bring into being an unbalanced biochemistry that seeks equilibrium. This self-created disharmony sets the body against itself, the mind against itself and the soul against itself. This internal discord is our fall from grace and Eden.

Each emotion comes with its own polarity, belief system, overruling objective, physiological effect and chemical signature as emotions are modes of perception that utilize different faculties of the mind, body and spirit. These modes of being make us think, feel and perceive the world in a very specific manner.

The modes of emotion include cognitive appraisal or perception, expressive behaviour, physiological arousal and subjective experience. These emotional modes are states of mind that make us think in a particular way that is beneficial to the social group that we have identified with and are part of.

In essence, we become a social animal when under the influence of emotion and it is from our lower emotional animal nature that we have come to think of ourselves as social animals that have evolved over time.

The animal kingdom is governed and moved predominantly by their emotional and sensed nature. Emotions were never meant to be our primary guidance mechanism as we have the faculties of the higher mind such as insight, intellect, intuition and inspiration.

Religion has long warned us about the dangers and pitfalls of carnal emotion in which Christianity terms *'Sin'*. Within the teachings of Christianity, the seven deadly sins are all emotions and some refer to them as devils and spirits which Jesus cast out of the sick. In Buddhism, the three poisons are the effects of emotion (aversion & attachment) and their impact upon the mind (ignorance).

The effects of emotion come in and out of existence in accordance to the sine wave. The origin of the word *'sin'* comes from the word *'sine'* which means *'to miss the mark'* and sine is the wave function of this dualistic sensed universe of motion.

The Wheel of Emotion

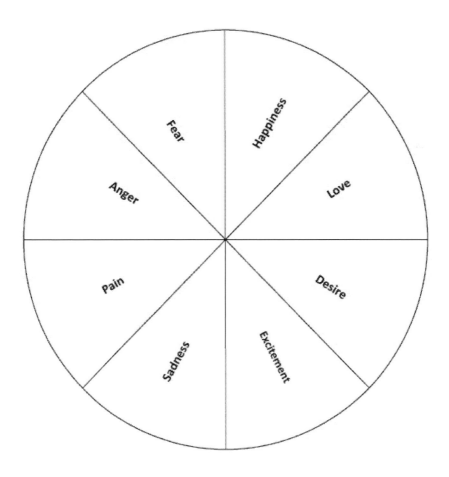

Fig 1. The 8 basic emotions and their pairing
in relation to their opposites.

Chapter 2

Rest

Rest is the cessation of emotion. From unrest emotion comes into being. Emotion is energy manifesting as action. The emotional man forever moves to find rest within a normal range which we term as *'Homeostasis'*.

Homeostasis is imperative to the notion of stress and most of our biological processes aim to achieve homeostasis and equilibrium within the body. This steady state is based on predetermined chemical set points and perceived limitations that are met when we satisfy our daily needs. We never maintain this steady state due to external and internal factors which disrupt homeostasis. This disruption to the steady state is what we deem as *'Stress'*.

Stress

There are three aspects of stress that correspond to the threefold aspects of consciousness.

1. *Physical stress* is the tension that arises from bodily sensation and the contact of our vehicle (body) with the outside objective world of motion and its effect upon our chemistry.

2. *Mental stress* is the tension that arises from the mental impressions of the sensed physical forms upon our mind and their effect upon our chemistry.

3. **Emotional stress** is the tension that arises from the energetic feelings that arise from identifying with the sensed mental impressions of the external world and their effect upon our chemistry.

All of what we consciously experience in life is related to feeling. Hearing, seeing, smelling, touching and tasting are all feelings, they are all but sensed impressions of the universe. Our ears feel sound waves when we hear, our eyes feel light waves when we see, our skin feels light waves when we touch, our nose feels light waves when we smell and our tongue feels light waves when we taste.

What we imagine mentally is done through our inner sense of sight and what we hear internally is heard through our inner ear. In esoteric circles these are known as the *'third eye'* and *'inner ear'*.

In Psychology, the Biopsychosocial Model of Stress proposes that stress is threefold. It states that there is an internal aspect, an external aspect and an interaction between the two. These three aspects are directly linked to the above categorisations of stress.

Physical Stress

The external element of stress can be brought on by a broad range of psychosocial stimuli that interrupt homeostasis and are seen as emotionally or physiologically threatening. It is the environmental conditions that trigger the acknowledgement of stress that can lead to the stress response.

Emotional Stress

The internal aspect of stress includes a set of physiological and neurological responses to stress. Endocrinologist Hans Selye defined this response as the *'General Adaptation Syndrome'* (GAS). The GAS response to stress is seen as a response that triggers the organism's resources to cope with an imminent threat.

This internal conditioned response to external conditions is what we perceive as stressful and arouses the fight-or-flight response. Selye found that when someone is subjected to persistent stress the subject goes through three stages: - Alarm Reaction, Resistance and Exhaustion. These three stages of GAS highlight the negative cycle of tension-release that is involved in negative emotions and arousal.

__The alarm reaction__ is the fear half of the fight-or-flight response that involves numerous physiological and neurological reactions to a stressor. When we perceive something as a threat the pituitary gland and sympathetic nervous system (SNS) receive a signal from the hypo-thalamus. The SNS then prompts the adrenal glands to produce corticosteroids which increase energy output through metabolism. Adrenocorticotrophic hormone (ACTH) is released by the pituitary gland which stimulates the adrenal glands to produce noradrenaline and adrenaline extending the fight-or-flight response.

__The stage of resistance__ is the anger half of the fight-or-flight response and is a prolonged state of arousal that occurs if the threat is not removed. If the stressful situation persists increased hormones further disrupt homeostasis damaging internal organs and leaving us prone to illness.

The exhaustion stage happens after continuous resistance. During this stage disintegration occurs as the body's energy reserves have been depleted. This stage is secondary to the pain caused to the subject carrying the anger and is the release half of the tension-release cycle of emotions and what we know as *'sadness'*. The exhaustion stage offers a rest bite period so the body can replete its energy stores and repair itself.

Mental Stress

Mental stress (also known as *'Psychological stress'*) is the interplay between the internal and external aspects of stress that include the individual's cognitive faculties of reason. According to the Cognitive-relational model of stress (also known as the *'Transactional theory of stress'*) for an event to be stressful or threatening, it must first be perceived as such. The cognitive faculties of appraisal are key to assessing whether a situation is threatening, equates to harm/loss or is deemed a challenge. These processes appraise the significance and relevance of the event based on a person's subjective evaluation which is based on one's previous experiences, resources and self-image.

The Cognitive-relational model states that an individual's appraisal of a situation is more important to psychological well-being than the presence of stress itself. The appraisal of stress is twofold according to this model and includes primary and secondary appraisal. Primary appraisal entails discerning whether or not an event is deemed as stressful, irrelevant or beneficial. If deemed as stressful, the situation is then appraised as either a challenge (the possibility of achievement, growth or reward), a threat (something that may bring about harm or loss), or harm or loss (damage or injury that has already occurred).

Each classification produces a different emotional reaction in relation to the cycle of emotions as the classification of stress is based on prior conditioning, past experiences and learned behaviours. Harm or loss stressors give rise to pain or sadness and are the motivating force behind the cycle of negative emotions. Threatening stressors elicit fear, anger and anxiety while challenging stressors produce excitement or desire when one thinks and feels they can overcome such challenges.

After the initial appraisal of whether or not the situation is deemed as a challenge or threat, secondary appraisal takes place in which we evaluate our resources and ability to cope with the stressor. It is only when a specific event is deemed significant to our life and there is a perceived mismatch between a situation's demands and our ability to overcome them that stress occurs.

Positive and Negative Stress

Hans Selye in the 1970s proposed a model dividing stress into two categories, eustress and distress. Selye stated that stress that improves mental or physical function was referred to as *'eustress'* while continuous stress that was persistent and unresolved via coping or adaptation was labelled as *'distress'*. The differences in experience, individual expectations and ability and resources to deal with the imagined or real stress resulted in either eustress or distress.

Later renditions to the Cognitive-relational model of stress state that when a situation or event is appraised as a threat or harm/loss, it creates only negative emotions and if the event is considered a challenge, a different set of physiological responses occur, creating the potential for both positive and negative emotions.

Researchers have found that physiological reactions to stressors depend on two components: effort and distress. Studies suggest that there are three categories of physiological reactions to stressors which are: -

1) **Effort with distress** is the response to everyday struggles that is experienced as negative emotion. The stressor is perceived as a threat or harm/loss and there is an increase in the secretion of cortisol and catecholamines.

2) **Effort without distress** is the reaction to a situation appraised as a challenge and is experienced as a positive emotion. This type of physiological reaction suppresses cortisol secretion whilst increasing the secretion of catecholamines.

3) **Distress without effort** is a pattern of behaviour that often shows up in people who are suffering from depression that fosters feelings of helplessness and passivity. Cortisol secretion increases with a moderate increase in catecholamines.

Arousal

Stress whether it is deemed positive or negative motivates us into action through the arousal of the sympathetic nervous system and its general action to mobilise the body for either the fight-or-flight or the excite-or-approach response.

The major neural systems implicated in ascending arousal begin in the brainstem and project to the cerebral cortex. The major neural systems are collectively known as the arousal system and are centred around the brain's neurotransmitters; dopamine, serotonin, acetylcholine, noradrenaline and histamine.

Acetylcholine is associated with anger and muscle activity, noradrenaline with general arousal and dopamine with focus, reward and attention. Serotonin is implicated in positive appraisal, perception and movement, while histamine acts in a similar manner to noradrenaline and is involved in wakefulness.

The four basic emotions of ascending arousal are fear, excitement, anger and desire which are related to the specific states of arousal: -

- Sexual or passionate arousal - Lust/sexual desire
- Predatory arousal - Anger and desire
- Negative arousal - Fear & distress
- Positive arousal - Excitement & eustress

The ascending arousal states activate the sympathetic nervous system into action and work in opposition to the parasympathetic nervous system which promotes rest and a return to homeostasis. It is from these ascending arousal neural pathways and their related emotions that the tension half of the tension-release cycle is set in motion.

There are however, descending arousal pathways which counteract and work in opposition to the ascending pathways. One such pathway is the Gamma-Aminobutyric acid (GABA) pathway which interrupts arousal and wakefulness and has been implicated in positive mood states and the modulation of negative emotions.

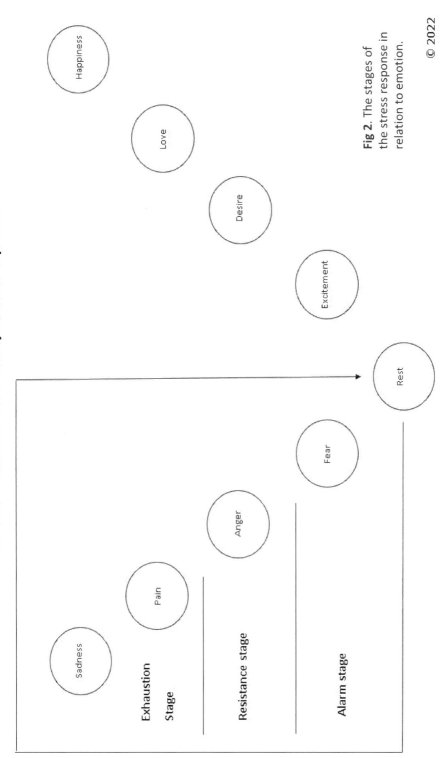

Emotion in relation to Hans Selye's GAS response

Fig 2. The stages of the stress response in relation to emotion.

© 2022

Chapter 3

Excitement

Excitement is a positive emotion of up-regulatory arousal
that directly contributes to the intensity of desire. It is a
positive emotion of input arousal that fuels the output
emotion of arousal which we know as desire.

In the field of psychology, excitement is also known as
'anticipation' and in physics it parallels that state of an
atom that has an increased energy level above the baseline
norm and is referred to as *'excitation'* or an *'excited state'*.

Excitement is arousal defined as pleasant without the
added force or pressure being exerted upon us; it is what
Selye refers to as *'eustress'*. With excitement we welcome
the stimulus as it is not perceived as a threat but still arouses
us. Excitement parallels intense interest and motivates the
attraction response as it supplies the drive that attracts us
to seek comfort, pleasure and wholeness.

Excitement is an increase in stress that is appraised
positively with the anticipation of something good. We
see ourselves and the environment in a positive light.
Excitement is an eager response expressing how deeply
we want to experience that which has stimulated or
excited us in a pleasant manner.

When a new stimulus arouses and excites us, we pay
attention to it because we understand that it relates to
our happiness and survival. If the stimulus did not relate
to our survival in some shape or form, we would move
on and tend to the things that are relevant to our lives.

Excitement is the anticipation part in the excite-or-approach response to our environment and the stimuli within it. With excitement there is no perceived mismatch between object and subject as we consciously identify with or get relief from that which has excited us.

The experience of excitement is labelled as pleasant and enjoyable as opposed to excitements apparent opposite fear. Fear and excitement however, are two sides of the same coin as they are of the same whole. Excitement is the positive invert of fear and fear is the negative invert of excitement as the polarity of each emotion is in the opposite direction.

Fear and excitement share the same neural circuitry for facial expression, physiological effects on the body and arousal but are appraised differently due to differences in neural activity, experience and neurochemistry. Some of the physiological effects of excitement are the same as fear but appraised positively. The pleasurable traits that accompany excitement may be due to the release of catecholamines and other feel-good neurochemicals such as serotonin and phenylethylamine that inhibit negative emotions and are involved in positive mood states.

Personality types associated with people who are easily excitable are predominantly sanguine. People with a sanguine temperament tend to be extroverted, sociable and pleasure-seeking.

Neurochemistry & Physiology

Excitement activates the ascending reticular-activating system (ARAS) of the brain which regulates the endocrine and autonomic nervous systems, attention, arousal and wakefulness.

The ARAS regulates two forms of arousal. The first type is predominantly cholinergic and involves acetylcholine (ACH). It encourages purposeful intentional action that depends on information from other areas of the brain and is implicated in anger and desire. The second type of arousal involves the adrenergic part of the ARAS and is largely related to the noradrenergic neurons of the locus coeruleus. This type of arousal is associated with fear and excitement and is involved in basic responses such as defecation, urination, ejaculation and vocalisation.

Some of the physiological effects of excitement include increases in sensory alertness, attention, movement, blood pressure and heart rate. The main neurotransmitters involved in excitement are dopamine, glutamate, adrenaline, noradrenaline, phenylethylamine (PEA) and serotonin.

PEA stimulates the pleasurable experience of excitement and is known as the *'excitant amine'*. PEA arouses feelings of exhilaration, joyfulness, euphoria and attraction and has been linked to the regulation of mood, physical energy and attention. PEA has a class of drugs named after it due to its psychoactive properties. Recreational drugs such as 3, 4-methylenedioxymethamphetamine (MDMA) and mescaline belong to this class of drugs and studies have found that PEA increases energy and can be found in chocolate.

PEA stimulates the release of dopamine and noradrenaline and has been implicated in headaches, attention deficit hyperactivity disorder (ADHD) and the antidepressant effects of exercise. Taken in high doses, PEA can produce typical behaviour similar to that of amphetamine. High levels of PEA are associated with schizophrenia, while low levels are found in those suffering from ADHD, depression and autism.

Noradrenaline is another neurotransmitter implicated in arousal and deficiencies in noradrenaline have been found to be linked with low levels of interest, excitement, impaired memory and loss of alertness. These symptoms are common in numerous psychiatric conditions such as ADHD and depression and why some medications aim to increase noradrenaline levels.

Moderate increases in noradrenaline create a heightened sense of arousal that is pleasurable and several recreational drugs such as caffeine, amphetamines and cocaine work by raising the level of noradrenaline giving the user that feel good experience. Studies suggest that some people using Selective Noradrenaline Reuptake Inhibitors (SNRI's) develop an increased sense of physical and emotional arousal.

High levels of noradrenaline have been found to produce a state of arousal that is unpleasant and creates fear, anxiety, jumpiness, irritability and restlessness. Extreme and abrupt increases in noradrenaline can cause panic attacks. In the fight-or-flight response excesses of adrenaline and noradrenaline are made to give us the extra strength and energy that is needed to deal with the threat at hand.

Serotonin is associated with energetic arousal and positive mood states and is involved in the regulation of wakefulness, appetite, mood and muscle contractions. Low levels of serotonin have been shown to be correlated with lower energy levels, depression and anxiety. Anti-depressants such as Selective Serotonin Re-uptake Inhibitors (SSRI'S) alleviate depression and negative mood states as they act on the brain's serotonergic synapses increasing levels of serotonin in the brain. Studies have shown that increases in serotonin in the neocortex appears to influence a positive bias towards the self and environment however, excesses in serotonin can cause hypomania, headaches, nausea and mental confusion.

Perception & Modality

Objectively excitement wants us to have more to gravitate towards that which we value and believe will make us happier as excitement plants the seed of motivation in the mind to seek and enjoy the object that we identify with.

On some level we identify with an aspect of ourselves that we have given away through the act of sex and aim to reintegrate it into who we are and it is through the act of orgasmic ejaculatory sex that we give away part of ourselves, chemically and energetically. Chemically we create an imbalance that perpetuates the cycle of addiction and we become attached to people, places and things that represent aspects of ourselves.

The things that excite us emotionally represent growth and expansion in some shape or form and we become excited at the chance of reunion with that which we have lost and reflects who we are in totality. Excitement gives purpose to desire to engage in and to go toward the object of our attention. There is no perceived mismatch between object and subject as we see ourselves and environmental stimuli in a positive light. We become enlivened with the possibility of getting our next chemical fix through the feeling the object of desire elicits within us and we become excited with the anticipation of the thing that brings us joy and/or relief.

Excitement is appraised positively as it contributes to our happiness in some shape or form and through repetition we condition our bodies to become dependent on such things to make us feel happy and to maintain homeostasis.

When we are emotionally excited the brain fills in the missing gaps and our rationality diminishes. Excitement magnifies the object of desire into something bigger than it actually is and we are often let down by things as they do not live up to our expectations of what we imagined them to be.

The way we process information and integrate it regarding fear and excitement are one and the same. Excitement has an inverted effect on the person experiencing it to that of fear as excitement magnifies and exaggerates the qualities we deem positive. Thoughts are more frequent when we are excited as arousal and sensory input is heightened.

The Negative and Positive Cycles of Emotion

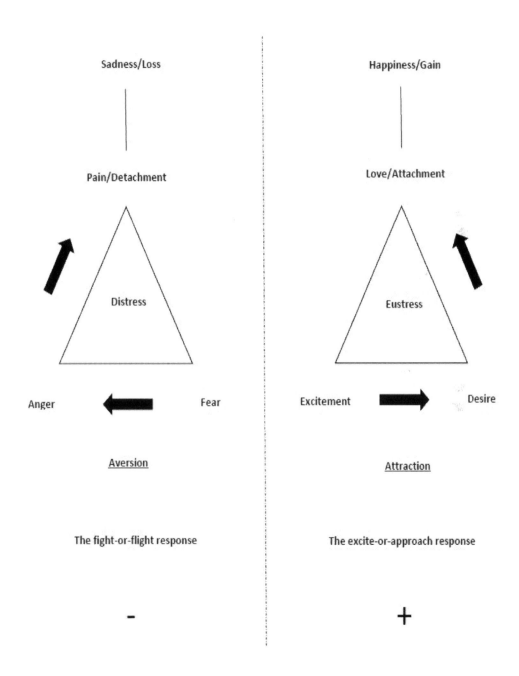

Fig 3. The fight-or-flight and the excite-or-approach responses mirror one another for either attraction to that which you see as a gain or aversion to that which you see as a loss.

Chapter 4

Fear

Fear is an emotional response to a perceived threat or danger. It is an intense aversion to, or apprehension of a person, place, event, activity or object. In Hans Selye's GAS response to stress, fear occurs in the alarm stage and is the flight half of the fight-or-flight response.

The emotion is a negative and unpleasant reaction to a real or imaged threat of danger that is distressing. Fear is an unpleasant response to a social or external pressure that expresses how intensely we do not want to experience the possibility of harm or loss.

Pain, loss and negative self-image are the driving forces behind fear and we learn how and what to be fearful of as fear is a conditioned learned response. The arousal of fear is stressful and uncomfortable so we remove ourselves from the threat at hand and the uncomfortable feelings that accompany it.

Fear is an input emotion of up-regulatory arousal that directly contributes to the output emotion of anger. The objective of fear is avoidance and it has an inverted effect on the person experiencing it to that of excitement as fear is a state of being emotionally aroused that is appraised negatively with the anticipation of loss or harm.

When we are fearful, we respect the threat at hand but doubt our ability and resources to cope with it. There is a perceived mismatch between a situation's demands and our ability to deal with the threat at hand or the possibility of loss. We experience this mismatch as a social force or pressure that puts us in our place in relation to the group or others.

Fear is often distinguished from anxiety which typically occurs without any external threat however, the mind reacts the same way to what it perceives internally via memory & imagination and externally via the senses. The amygdala is activated when we react to an imagined or real threat as the brain cannot tell the difference between a real or imagined threat.

Excitement and fear are two sides of the same coin as they are of the same whole. Fear is the negative invert of excitement and excitement is the positive invert of fear as the polarity of each emotion is in the opposite direction. Each emotion shares the same neural circuitry for facial expression, physiological effects on the body and arousal but are appraised differently due to differences in neural activity, experience and neurochemistry.

Some of the physiological effects of fear are the same as excitement but appraised negatively. The undesirable traits that accompany fear may be due to the release of cortisol and other neurochemicals such as noradrenaline and glutamate that are involved in negative emotions and unpleasant arousal. The neurochemistry involved in the stress response counteracts and depletes the body of feel-good chemicals such as serotonin and endorphins which are required to inhibit and modulate the stress response in the higher cortex.

Neurochemistry & Physiology

Fear is one half of the fight-or-flight response that is characterised by an increase in heart rate and muscle tension with fluctuations in breathing rate and depth that enable us to escape from danger. Blood is pushed from the gut to other parts of the body such as the legs aiding the transfer of nutrients, heat and oxygen and sometimes the body freezes giving us time to think about what the best plan of action is.

When a fear stimulus occurs unexpectedly, we become startled and jumpy. The expression of fear with the widening of the eyes and dilated pupils allows us to search our environment so we can identify the threat at hand. When we receive auditory, visual or sensory stimuli that is identified as a possible threat, information is sent to the amygdala which triggers the hypothalamus to produce Corticotropin-releasing factor (CRF). The increase in CRF signals the pituitary gland to release Adrenocorticotropic hormone (ACTH) which triggers the adrenal glands to produce cortisol and increase the production of glucose supplying the essential energy needed for flight. Information received from the senses is sent to the neocortex via the amygdala and the amygdala will then either continue or abort the stress response depending on the information it receives.

The amygdala controls the first physical response to stress along with the hypothalamus and is connected to the hippocampus and neocortex. The hippocampus is known for its role in storing long-term memories. Research indicates that the hippocampus encourages emotional behaviour that is relevant to its social context and people with damage to the hippocampus sometimes display emotions that are irrelevant at a particular time and place. People who suffer from post-traumatic stress disorder (PTSD) experience abrupt, intense emotional reactions to quite innocent stimuli such as war veterans who panic or suddenly cry when a car backfires.

Memories of a traumatic experience can persist long after a stressful event and damage to the prefrontal cortex makes fear difficult to suppress. In healthy individuals the left prefrontal cortex helps to inhibit the stress responses, while in depressed people the left prefrontal cortex shows the greatest signs of damage. The amygdala has been shown to be overactive in people suffering from depression too however, this over reactivity is reduced considerably in those who take antidepressants.

ACTH, CRF, cortisol, noradrenaline and adrenaline are some of the main neurochemicals involved in the fear response along with dopamine and glutamate. The route in which the brain processes fear increases the rate of noradrenergic activity in the locus coeruleus, which in turn activates the sympathetic nervous system increasing the release of adrenaline and noradrenaline from the adrenal glands.

The released noradrenaline floods the brainstem, limbic system and neocortex putting the brain on edge. The main effect of noradrenaline is to increase the general reactivity of the brain making us more sensitive and aware of our environment. Thoughts are more frequent when the sensory circuits are overloaded as sensory information is brought to our attention so we can discern what the best plan of action is. The amygdala and hippocampus prompt the release of dopamine resulting in an increase in attention and focus

on the threat at hand while getting our muscles ready for
action.

Comparison of some of the physiological effects of fear and excitement.

Fear	Excitement
Increased heart rate	Increased heart rate
Sympathetic nervous system activation	Sympathetic nervous system activation
Increased blood pressure	Increased blood pressure
Increased energy	Increased energy
Increased sensory alertness	Increased sensory alertness
Negative sensory overload	Positive sensory overload
Pupils dilated	Pupils dilated
Ascending reticular activating system – Adrenergic	Ascending reticular activating system – Adrenergic
Increased thoughts	Increased thoughts
Increased imagination	Increased imagination
Amygdala activation	Amygdala activation

Perception & Modality

Fear has the primary purpose of removing the threat of danger through avoidance. We perceive the stressors and our ability to overcome them in a negative way. When in full flight, we perceive stimuli in our environment as a possible threat and by its very nature the flight response hijacks our rational mind and catapults us into *'avoidance'* mode. We aim to remove ourselves from the situation as the experience is uncomfortable and unpleasant as there is a perceived mismatch between the situation's demands and our ability to cope with it.

Fear like excitement gives us a heightened sense of awareness and keeps us alert. When presented with a new situation it is better to be alert and attentive than docile and diligent. We process information faster when we are outside of our comfort zone as we are more aware of the possible dangers ahead. Once we become desensitised and familiar to the situation our stress levels are reduced as we become aware that there is no impending threat or danger.

Fear is full of cognitive distortions as we selectively attend to the threat at hand and our ability to think logically is compromised as we are driven by past experiences and the possibility of what might happen in the future. Fear does not bring confidence with it but rather it sensitises us to pain and the perceived threat. The mind's ability to make rational decisions is greatly compromised when in fear as our awareness is primarily focused on loss and pain.

When we are fearful, we direct our attention to short-term survival and do not think about the long-term consequences of our actions and beliefs. We find it difficult to make sound choices in that moment because of the body's chemistry and its effect upon our mind. It is near impossible to remain positive when we are stuck in survival mode as our hearts and minds are not open as we perceive almost everything in our environment in a negative light including ourselves. We see everything and everyone as a possible enemy and overreact to minor things as our fear is blown out of proportion and thinking becomes distorted. We see the world through the filter of probable danger as we limit our focus to the things that could harm us.

Fear brings us uncertainty, doubt and confusion. When we are fearful, we are bombarded with memories of previous painful experiences and we become pessimistic as we imagine the possible negative outcomes. Negative thoughts flood the mind and put us on edge as the balance of neurochemicals are tipped in favour of cortisol and other stress-related chemicals.

Our minds run overtime when we are fearful and our thoughts are purely negative. The duration of thought is shorter, but the frequency of thoughts are quicker as we scan the environment and memory reserves for possible dangers. We cannot think straight and assume the worst of a given situation when we are in fear as fear magnifies the perceived object making it more of a threat than it actually is, keeping us in a perpetual state of alarm.

The processing of fear is heavily based on our imagination, presumption and past experiences. When we are fearful, we know our thinking is distorted and what actually happens in real life rarely matches up to what we think will happen. Fear is based on a flaw of presumption because it goes off previous experiences and guess work. The acronym of fear sums it up really well - False Evidence Appearing Real. Fear simultaneously sharpens and dulls our memories and we lose the ability to enjoy ourselves as we lack the internal chemistry needed to feel good. When we think we are in danger, we seek comfort and safety in familiarity.

Fear is one of the main emotions we try to escape using various psychoactive substances and sensed pleasures as a way of feeling better and readdressing the chemical imbalance within. For some, indulging in sensed pleasures as a form of self-medicating seems to be their only option to alleviate the fear and anxiety that they face in life. Fear is one of the most obvious examples of how our thoughts and feelings lie to us and how inextricably linked they are.

The input and output cycles of emotion

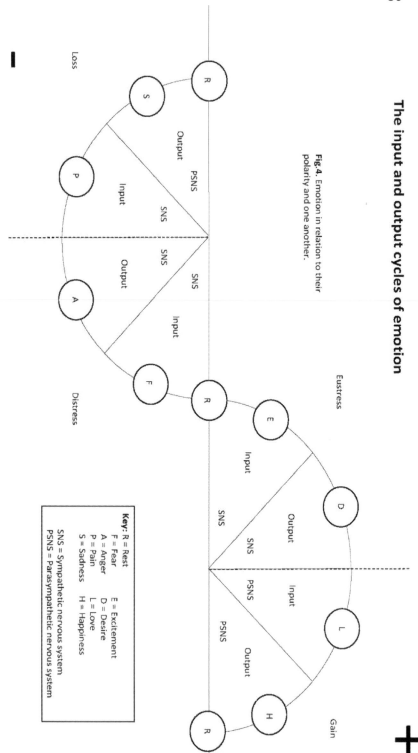

Fig. 4. Emotion in relation to their polarity and one another.

Key: R = Rest
F = Fear   E = Excitement
A = Anger   D = Desire
P = Pain   L = Love
S = Sadness   H = Happiness

SNS = Sympathetic nervous system
PSNS = Parasynpathetic nervous system

Chapter 5

Anger

Anger is a negative emotion that is commonly expressed in response to a dangerous, threatening, unpleasant, irritating or frustrating stimulus and is the resilience to a perceived threat of harm or loss.

In Hans Selye's GAS response to stress, anger occurs in the resistance stage to a stressor and is the fight half of the fight-or-flight response. Anger is the feeling of dissatisfaction or animosity that is aroused by a real or imagined threat or offence to that which we are emotionally attached to, accompanied by the urge to do harm.

We become angry when we feel we have been mistreated or discriminated against, lost something we value, are judged in a negative way, or someone questions our worth. Anger is aroused by the sense of having been wronged, offended or denied and the causes of our anger are typically found in the controllable and intentional characteristics of someone else's actions.

Anger gives us purpose, drive and focus and is arousal defined as unpleasant. Anger is an output emotion of up-regulatory arousal that is fuelled by the input emotion of fear and is the tension half of the tension-release cycle of emotion. Anger is objective, discriminative, decisive, judgemental, critical and unforgiving and is secondary to pain but at the same time can be the cause of it.

The objective of anger is to discharge, belittle, suppress or oppress the opposition so they are no longer a threat to our wellbeing or status quo. We push away that which we don't want and see in a negative light.

Anger and desire are two sides of the same coin as they are of the same whole. Anger is the negative invert of desire and desire is the positive invert of anger as the polarity of each emotion is in the opposite direction. Desire is *'to want'* and anger is *'to not want'*. Anger repels that which we do not want and perceive as a threat or loss, while desire attracts that which we want and see as a comfort or gain.

Desire and anger share similar neural circuitry for facial expression, physiological effects on the body and arousal but are appraised differently due to differences in neuro-chemistry, neural activity and experience. The negative traits that accompany anger may be due to the lack of serotonin and other feel-good chemicals that regulate and inhibit the stress response.

The choleric temperament is associated with anger and is sometimes referred to as the *'angry temperament'*. People with this temperament tend to use anger and desire as their coping mechanisms when in tight situations. Choleric personality types are typically outgoing, task orientated, ambitious, quick tempered, critical and judgmental. They have leadership qualities and reserves of passion and energy that help them achieve their desired goals.

Neurochemistry & Physiology

With anger the muscles tense up and we assume a squared-off position ready for defensive action or an attack. Increases in muscle tension give us strength and confidence when the skeletal and facial muscles become active. Blood rushes to the hands when we are angry enabling us to strike out or wield a weapon and the face flushes as blood flows to the limbs, preparing us for action. As the heart rate increases, the body (if injured) is at risk of bleeding to death, so blood is pulled away from the skin towards the bone to prevent this.

The release of catecholamines causes an increase in energy as adrenaline, noradrenaline and glucocorticoids are released by the adrenal cortex activating the sympathetic nervous system. Glucose released from the liver and muscles provides a burst of energy while at the same time our breathing rate, blood pressure and heart rate increase. Dopamine released by the adrenal medulla gives us confidence, drive and focus while the release of endorphins and noradrenaline help us deal with the possibility of pain.

When we are angry, our eyes dilate and brow muscles turn downward and inward as we fixate on the target of aggression. Our nose wrinkles as our nostrils flare and the jaw clenches as the lips tighten up. We pay attention to nothing else other than our target of aggression as tunnel vision takes over. Our attention narrows and fixates on the object of negative affection as the ascending reticular activating system filters out irrelevant stimuli.

The neurochemistry that anger induces energises and strengthens the body while the release of endorphins stop pain from affecting our ability to defend ourselves.

The neurochemicals involved in anger provide a lasting state of arousal. Among these chemicals are vasopressin, which is responsible for the increases in heart rate and blood pressure, adrenaline and noradrenaline which provide energetic arousal and acetylcholine and testosterone which get the muscles ready for action.

Psychologists have long thought that there are two adaptive functions of anger that are represented in two separate neurological pathways in the brain. The first is commonly associated with defensive anger which is a response to loss, danger or a threat and the second function is associated with consummatory predatory anger which is in fact desire. The first path alerts the thalamus-amygdala system and this type of anger is reactive. We learn how to control this type of anger early on in life and trouble with it results in problems with expression and temperament. This route is quicker than the second path that relays information to the neocortex via the limbic system and hypothalamus. The second path is more analytical in nature and longer than the first path as it helps us think things through to get to the best desired outcome.

When we get what we want, the second stage does not activate the desire to consume as the objective is already achieved however, if we don't get what we want the brain can easily revert straight back to the fight-or-flight response. The subcortical nuclei of both pathways are near to each other. When one is turned on, the other is turned off as only one system can be activated at any time. A desire to want something and the frustration of meeting a resistance to that desire can result in rage. Once we get what we want however, the system moves on.

Tunnel vision and denial are common characteristics of anger as anger stops information from reaching other parts of the brain as endorphins shut down the neocortex. Anger impedes our ability to think critically as it shuts down sensory input so we selectively attend to information that supports why we are angry.

The neocortex helps keep our negative emotions in check as the prefrontal cortex deals with appraisal and judgments. The left prefrontal cortex regulates and inhibits negative emotions keeping things under control while the amygdala deals with emotional arousal.

When anger rages out of control surplus cortisol and adrenaline cause a set of destructive cellular reactions that can cause the brain to struggle with the overload of neurochemicals involved in the stress response. People prone to anger tend to experience events more stressful than usual as anger and stress fuel one another (anger and stress are the same thing).

ACTH released from the pituitary gland signals the adrenals to release corticosteroids which activates the fight-or-flight response. The brain receives feedback information from the corticosteroids to reduce the attack threshold and put us on edge. The stress of anger then further depletes us of serotonin and other feel-good chemicals creating more stress and more anger and the cycle of negativity continues.

Problems with anger are associated with coronary-artery disease, drug abuse, alcohol abuse and hypertension. Angry people tend to get ill often as chronic anger affects the immune system in a negative way. Anger has a negative impact on our health as acetylcholine in excess is a *'poison'* and triggers the release of substance P, the *'pain chemical'*.

Low levels of phenylethylamines are correlated with anger, anxiety and depression and studies have shown that anger triggers the dorsal anterior cingulate cortex (dACC), an area of the brain where pain, error detection and conflict are processed. The dACC has connections to many areas of the brain including the frontal cortex and is involved in the processing of anger which makes sense considering the motives behind anger are to protect us from pain and loss.

Perception & Modality

The modality of anger is to attack and to negatively deconstruct a person, situation or object with the aim of repelling that which you see in a negative light and do not want. When we are angry, we see things in such a way as to find faults, weaknesses, flaws and imperfections with the objective of harming or pushing away the perceived threat or loss. While fear exaggerates the perceived dangers, anger downplays them and makes them less. Anger devalues an object, event or situation that we see as a threat and rejects its impact or importance.

Anger fools us into thinking we have control over a situation or object however, when we are angry, we experience a perceptual loss in objective observability and our ability to self-monitor is compromised. If we really had control, there would be no need for anger. The fact that anger has been elicited within us demonstrates a lack of control. Anger along with desire gives us a false sense of worth, a lust for power and domination and a false sense of achievement or gain. On the chemical level we have gained something from anger the release of endorphins and an adrenaline rush. This false sense of achievement however, only feeds the brains appetite for destruction and reinforces its addictive nature by masking how we are truly feeling and the reality of the situation.

We become accustomed to the release of endorphins when we are angry which gives us a false sense of control and feeds our denial that we have a problem with anger in the first place. We justify our actions with some false pretence as the over arousal of adrenaline and noradrenaline reduces our capacity to recall the details of our anger. It is difficult for us to remember the details of a heated argument as it takes a while for us to calm down. During this time, we could easily become angered by minor things that would not normally cause us to get angry as the brain is very efficient at spotting an opportunity to get its next neurochemical fix no matter the cost.

Anger is full of perceptual biases and cognitive distortions. It is a very basic, animalistic emotion that is dumb at the best of times as dogmatic thinking takes over as endorphins shut down the neocortex. Thoughts are less frequent and last longer as our attention is focused on the enemy and our ability to process complex thoughts is severely reduced.

When we are in danger we need to act immediately as over consideration and doubt could get us killed. Anger limits our capacity to think deeply as it shuts down sensory input, so we selectively attend to information that supports our reasons to be angry. We think only on a discriminatory two-factor basis - black/white, good/bad, enemy/ally and reject any information that goes against our reasoning while filtering out any harmful stimuli. Anger is short-sighted, confident and dumb. Tunnel vision deludes an angry person as they only see what they want to see and this is particularly evident in denial where we reject any information that does not justify our anger.

With anger there are no winners - it is a lose-lose situation. If anger is expressed outwardly, we give it away to someone or something else and if suppressed it works against us. The objective of anger remains the same whether that anger is turned inward or expressed outwardly and the longer anger is suppressed, the stronger it becomes as it engulfs the neocortex.

Suppressing anger for long periods of time is a form of self-harm as the objective of anger is to cause harm or prevent loss. Without expression, mental, physical and emotional problems occur. Anger can eat away at you like a virus, disrupting your immune system, it distorts your perception of reality and of yourself. Instead of loathing others, you begin to loathe yourself as the anger grows in strength and takes over the desire not to cause harm.

Anger causes physical and emotional pain in an attempt to protect us/the ego from harm or loss by means of transference. We pass on the effect of pain (anger) to others, usually the people we are closest to such as friends and family or those we look down on and think we are better than. When anger is suppressed for long periods of time or directed toward the self it causes the suppressor to generate self-perpetuating emotional pain that is often self-medicated. This in turn leads to more stress and frustration, leading to more anger and pain and the cycle of negative emotions keeps itself going.

The use of drugs to deal with the emotional pain can cause a physical strain on the body and lead to physical pain and poor health. We react the same way to physical pain as we do to emotional pain as the brain cannot tell the difference between the two. When we hurt ourselves physically, we tense up and become angry as a resistance to the fact that we have hurt ourselves which in turn helps mask the actual pain caused.

Anger causes pain and protects the ego from it as anger is secondary to pain but at the same time can be the cause of pain. In the grieving process we often go through a stage of denial as this is our natural tendency to avoid pain. As the pain grows, we become angry and resist the fact that we have lost someone close to us until we accept the loss and move on. The true emotions that fuel anger are love and pain for if we had nothing to fear or nothing to lose, then anger would seem pointless.

Neural pathways in relation to chemistry and emotion

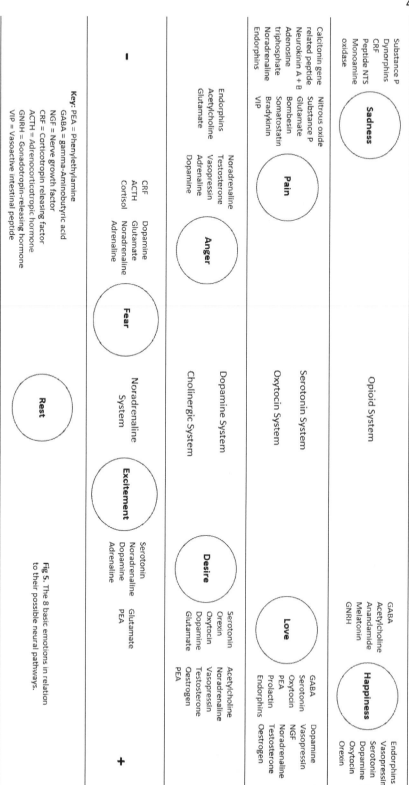

Fig 5. The 8 basic emotions in relation to their possible neural pathways.

Key: PEA = Phenylethylamine
GABA = gamma-Aminobutyric acid
NGF = Nerve growth factor
CRF = Corticotropin releasing factor
ACTH = Adrenocorticotropic hormone
GNRH = Gonadotropin-releasing hormone
VIP = Vasoactive intestinal peptide

Temperaments and Personality types in relation to emotion

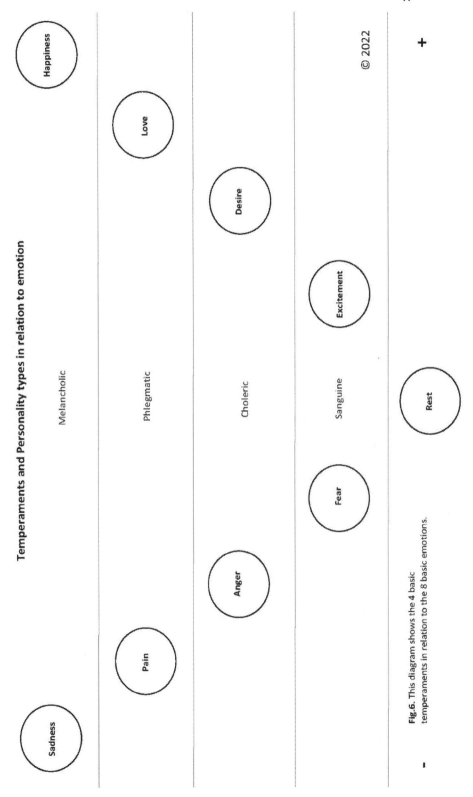

Fig.6. This diagram shows the **4 basic** temperaments in relation to the **8 basic emotions.**

© 2022

Chapter 6

Desire

Desire is the emotion *'to want'* and *'to crave'* that which
you see in a positive light and is a sense of yearning for a
person, place or object. Desire is the approach part of the
excite-or-approach response that provides us with the drive
to meet our needs of food, shelter, comfort and unity.

The desire for someone or something is aroused by a specific
stimulus that excited us in a pleasant manner. With desire
we become enlivened with the chance of union with that
which we see in a positive light. Desire keeps us connected
to our environment and those around us. Desire encourages
social development and growth, but sometimes our desires
can get us in trouble as desire is part of our mammalian
drives such as lust, thirst and hunger.

Although we see desire as a positive emotion, it is part of
greed, envy, gluttony and lust. The driving force behind
desire is the pursuit of pleasure with the intent to seek
that which we value and see in a positive light. Desire gives
us a sense of purpose, drive and ambition and is arousal
defined as pleasant so we are motivated to seek the object
of affection and value.

Desire is an output emotion of up-regulatory arousal
where we go to be stimulated that is fuelled by the input
emotion of excitement where the stimulation comes to us.
Excitement arouses us and desire identifies and focuses
on the object of affection. We welcome the arousal as it
pleasantly engages us in a perceived controlled manner.

With desire we see ourselves and the environmental stimuli in a positive light. There is no perceived mismatch between a situation's demands and our ability and resources to cope with it. We welcome the stimulus and deem it as a challenge as we see it as an opportunity for personal growth and gain. Desire is fuelled by what Hans Selye refers to as eustress in his GAS response to stress.

Anger and desire are two sides of the same coin as they are of the same whole. Desire is the positive invert of anger as it has an inverted effect on the person experiencing it to that of anger as the polarity is in the opposite direction. Desire is *'to want'* and anger is *'to not want'*. Desire is the attraction to that which we want and see as a comfort or gain while anger is the repulsion to that which we do not want and perceive as a threat or loss.

Desire and anger share similar neural circuitry for facial expression, physiological effects on the body and arousal but are appraised differently due to the differences in neurochemistry, neural activity and experience. Some of the physiological effects of desire are the same as anger but appraised positively. The positive traits that follow desire may be due to the release of serotonin and other feel-good chemicals that inhibit and quell negative emotions and are implicated in positive appraisal and arousal.

Neurochemistry & Physiology

Desire shares similar neurology and physiology as anger however, with anger the release of catecholamines is short and fast and with desire the release can be slow and gradual but without the elevated levels of cortisol.

The release of catecholamines cause an increase in energy as adrenaline, noradrenaline and glucocorticoids are released by the adrenal cortex arousing the sympathetic nervous system into action. As with exercise, the body warms up to the increases in adrenaline and the effects of desire are subtler with gradual increases in heart rate, temperature, blood pressure and breathing.

Dopamine released by the adrenal medulla provides a keen focus and a sense of purpose. The facial expressions of desire are similar to those of anger, but without the tensing of the jaw or clenching of teeth. The eyes dilate and the brow muscles move downward and inward as we fixate on the object of desire.

Desire is initiated by the brain via the ascending reticular activating system (ARAS). The ARAS transmits messages to the limbic system and hypothalamus relaying information from the senses. The ARAS along with other areas of the brain focus only on the relevant stimuli as we become fixated on the object of desire but with less intensity as the route in which desire takes can be longer and more cerebral in nature.

The amygdala and medial forebrain bundle are associated with appetite and desire and drive us to meet our basic needs such as warmth, coolness, food, water and sex partners. Desire is part of our appetitive needs that are reinforced by the brain's dopamine and serotonin reward systems. Food cravings for example, are the desire to eat specific foods, that are rich in either, carbohydrates, proteins or lipids with the aim of boosting the feel-good chemicals of the brain that promote growth or a return to homeostasis.

FMRI (functional magnetic resonance imaging) studies have shown that craving-related changes have been observed in the caudate, insula and hippocampus. These areas of the brain are reported to be involved in craving and the circuitry of love.

Serotonin, oxytocin, endorphins, dopamine, phenyle-thylamine and gamma-amino butyric acid are some of the main feel-good chemicals that are created or released due to the consumption of food and around 90% of serotonin is synthesised in the gut. Some of the same neurotransmitters and hormones involved in anger are released in desire. In anger and desire the catecholamine activation is more noradrenaline than adrenaline. In fear and excitement, the reverse is the case.

Vasopressin, testosterone, adrenaline, noradrenaline, acetylcholine, dopamine and oestrogen increase the arousal of desire (including sexual) but with the added benefit of a rise in feel-good chemicals such as serotonin and phenylethylamine which influence our experience and appraisal in a positive manner.

Desire like anger leads to the release of endorphins which reinforces the false sense of control that comes from both states of arousal. When we get what we want endorphins render the neocortex inoperative and we lose the ability to process complex thoughts. Endorphins shut down sensory input so we selectively attend to information that contributes to our feelings of pleasure and satisfaction.

Studies have found that dopamine and endorphins are the key to desire and stimulating the orbitofrontal cortex (OFC). The OFC is an area of the brain that is involved in reward association and pleasure. Dopamine desensitisation in the

OFC is associated with increased risk-taking behaviour similar to the behaviour found in people struggling with addictions and numerous studies have linked the neocortex with temptation, the inhibition of impulses and self-control.

Comparison of some of the physiological effects of anger and desire.

Anger	Desire
Increased heart rate	Increased heart rate
Sympathetic nervous system activation	Sympathetic nervous system activation
Increased blood pressure	Increased blood pressure
Increased energy	Increased energy
Filters sensory information	Filters sensory information
ARAS - Noradrenaline	ARAS - Noradrenaline
Increased temperature	Increased temperature
Tunnel vision	Tunnel vision
Amygdala activation	Amygdala activation
Keen focus	Keen focus
Eyes focused	Eyes focused
Muscle brows downward	Muscle brows downward
Eyebrows slanting inward	Eyebrows slanting inward
Increased breathing	Increased breathing
Increased attention span	Increased attention span
Decreased number of thoughts	Decreased number of thoughts

Perception & Modality

The objective of desire is the integration of energy and information into the self. Objectively desire brings the command to the forefront of awareness to want the thing that excited us in a pleasant manner. With desire we hold the object of affection in our minds until a union occurs and then we assess whether or not the experience was worth it. If our expectations are met, we aim to repeat the experience and if our expectations are not met, we feel let down, disappointed and move on.

The arousal of excitement brings a brief spike in pleasure which leads us to want and repeat the experience for a sustained period of time to reap the rewards. We integrate the things that please us into our lives to reap the benefits of the feelings that will derive from them and it is through this sense of achievement and gain that our sense of worth and control is confirmed. We feel special when we get what we want however, if we get what we want all the time our desires restrict our ability to think deeply as the brain shuts down sensory input so we selectively attend to information that supports our reasons to want that which we desire.

When we desire something, our thoughts are less frequent but last longer as our attention is mainly focused on the object of our affection and nothing else. Tunnel vision and denial are characteristics of desire. We see what we want to see irrelevant of the facts and accept no information that goes against our reasoning. We omit information that does not support our way of thinking and make high-risk/reward choices that sometimes have negative consequences.

The negative traits of desire are particularly evident in addiction as endorphins give us a false sense of worth and control. We deem that which we see in a positive light as a gain, which in turn prompts our denial that we have a problem in the first place. We justify our actions with some false pretence as the over arousal and increase in feel-good chemicals impede and interfere with our ability to remember details of past experiences and this significantly clouds our judgement. Our ability to make rational decisions is compromised as we are swayed by positive memories and biases toward that which we are emotionally attached to or chemically dependent on.

The modality of desire is to attract and to positively appraise a person, place, object or event to find strengths and ideals in the things that we desire, with the aim of gravitating toward that which we see in a positive light and brings us comfort or pleasure. For someone to desire someone or something, the object of affection must in some shape or form represent a part of our psyche that is missing and/or a feeling must derive from it. We desire the things that boost our sense of worth, make us feel special and provide comfort or release. We feel special when we have been discriminated for in the positive sense.

Desire gives us a false sense of worth and control and a lust for power, greed and domination. Desire gives us a sense that we have achieved something good and a gain has come from it. Chemically, we have gained something from desire, the release of endorphins and other feel-good chemicals that relieve our obsessive thoughts and comfort us.

We become attached to and dependent on those forms external to us that make us feel good and special, and in an attempt to quell the negativity and emptiness we feel inside, we self-medicate. We become attached to the things that represent that which we are lacking and have given away through the act of sex. Desire is the drive behind our obsession with possessions and materialism. Love-hate relationships are born out of our addiction to and dependency on others to feel worthwhile and whole again.

Desire is full of cognitive biases and perceptual distortions. We see the object of our affection in a positive light only finding strengths, ideals and perfections while ignoring any negative traits they may have. We see that which we are lacking in others and omit any information that goes against our reasoning. Desire is narrow-sighted and confident, it gives us drive, purpose and focus and is very decisive. Desire is discriminative and judgemental in the positive sense. We discriminate in the hope of a gain as desire promotes growth, unity and cooperation but only in the short term.

When under the influence of desire or anger we revert back to pack mentality and think only on a discriminatory two-factor basis. We see things as black/white, good/bad, enemy/ally and a sense of entitlement and righteous indignation are the result of desire. Desire-motivated aggression has been used for centuries to justify war or to coerce and bully others into doing things against their will. People ruled by anger and desire tend to subscribe to the philosophy that *'the end justifies the means'* and use terrible methods of achieving their goals.

Desire fools us into thinking we have perceived control over a situation or object however, when we desire and crave something, we experience a perceptual loss in objective observability and our ability to self-monitor is greatly reduced. If we truly had control, we would not crave and desire the other. The fact that a craving has been elicited within us clearly demonstrates a lack of control.

Chapter 7

Sex

Within the religious and esoteric practices of old and
new, rituals regarding sex have been and still are of great
importance. Sex magic, celibacy, tantra and chastity all
have their place in the religious and esoteric teachings
from around the world and some regard sex as *'original sin'*.

The etymological meaning of the word *'sex'* is derived from
the Latin *'secare'*, which means *'to cut off'* and hints at the
androgynous nature of the Soul as mentioned in ancient
texts. Some creation myths refer to sex when describing
how the universe came into being from the one primeval
parental force that divided itself to create offspring and the
forces of nature.

The Soul in its primordial state is androgynous and whole,
and it is through the act of sex that polarity and gender
come into being. Sex is not a thing itself but a condition
of a thing that manifests as gender on the physical plane.

All opposites in existence come into being through the
application of sex and every emotion that man experiences
is a result of sex. Sex is the one act that polarises the soul
and brings sin and suffering into being. Sex chemically
unbalances the mind and body. Sex sets the mind against
itself, the body against itself and the soul against itself.

*"And if a kingdom be divided against itself, that kingdom
cannot stand".* - Mark 3:24

A person can never be at peace with themselves as they are mentally at war with the idea of who they think they are, physically at war with their body as it forever seeks equilibrium and emotionally at war with their soul as it seeks the polarity it is lacking to be whole again.

The sexual energy of the universe is sometimes referred to as *'Christ energy'*, *'Life force'*, *'Qi'*, *'Chi'*, *'Prana'*, *'Kundalini'* or *'Spirit'* and is the creative principle of the universe. When the creative energy is let out or expelled it becomes the polar opposite and negative invert of itself, it becomes the destructive principle. Some refer to the destructive principle as the *'Kundabuffer'*, *'Satan's tail'*, *'Anti-Christ'* or *'Devil'* (which is lived spelled backwards).

Without sex, this dualistic sensed universe of motion and matter would not be. In Walter Russell's book *'The Secret of Light'* sex is defined as; -

"Sex is the division of a balanced equilibrium condition into two equally unbalanced conditions which negate each other periodically for the purpose of repeating the two unbalanced conditions"

"Every action of motion in the universe is a result of sex desire for motion from a state of rest, or for rest from a state of motion."

"The foundation of the physical universe is motion; the ever-changing motion arising out of pairs of unbalanced conditions which must forever move to seek the balanced stillness of unity from which they sprang as multiple pairs of units.

Unbalanced motion is the Negative Principle of instability, multiplicity and separateness which is this physical universe of electric octave waves of opposed lights.

In the Negative Principle there is no positive. It is composed entirely of pairs of negations which are forever voiding each other, canceling each other's action and reaction, thus negating each other by never allowing either one to exceed its fixed zero of universal stillness."

The Orgasm

Sex creates a neurochemical and hormonal imbalance within, in which we seek without, that which we have lost chemically and energetically (spiritually). It is through the act of orgasmic ejaculatory sex that we become chemically and spiritually incomplete. Within the teachings of Christianity, the orgasm is regarded as the forbidden fruit that Adam and Eve ate in the Garden of Eden that led to sin and suffering.

The orgasm that ejaculatory sex produces creates an overabundance of dopamine and other feel-good chemicals followed by an under abundance. As a result of the orgasm and its effect on dopamine levels, dopamine desensitisation occurs and sets in motion the cycles of emotions and addiction and in an attempt to address this chemical imbalance, we self-medicate. We engage in impulsive behaviours such as sex, drugs and junk food which give the brain a hit of dopamine. Addictions to sex, drugs, shopping, eating and gambling are all compulsions that are related to dopamine desensitisation.

Dopamine is at the centre of our desires, sexual or otherwise and all addictive substances stimulate the reward circuitry of the brain via the dopamine pathways. High levels of dopamine lead to compulsions and irrational behaviours that are not favourable to our survival. The arousal of engaging in pornography or the excitement of a new fling are examples of dopamine highs.

In evolutionary terms, some regard dopamine as the mechanism behind our need for supernormal stimuli. Most mammalian species however, evolved with specific estrus periods when they are ready to mate and when they are not *'in heat'* they are indifferent about sex. Humans on the other hand, don't seem to have mating seasons followed by long neutral periods toward sex when living in the lower mind. Instead, we have the possibility for continuous sexual cravings motivated by dopamine levels. We can manage our sexual desires as there is a built-in *'off switch'* that kicks in after too much arousal in which dopamine levels drop and prolactin levels rise.

After an orgasm, prolactin inhibits dopamine and acts as a *'sexual satiation'* hormone. It is not yet known how long prolactin suppresses dopamine for after an orgasm, but these highs and lows in dopamine and prolactin are the neurochemical cause of our addictive behaviours and shifts in perception. When we become sexually excited or aroused, dopamine and other feel-good chemicals increase, followed by a dip and we don't wait around for the passion cycle to correct itself because in effect it won't unless we reach enlightenment. We can however, boost low dopamine levels after an orgasm by reaching for the things that give us a dopamine hit. We can engage in more sex, junk food, drugs or drink to boost our dopamine levels.

High levels of stimulation, pleasure and sensation encourage high levels of dependency and habituation and we constantly shift from lows to new highs, never getting the chance to experience equilibrium again until we break the cycle of addiction and emotion. If animal studies on dopamine and addiction are anything to go by the passion cycle lasts for around two weeks. Researchers have found that in men the neurochemical changes last for at least seven days after ejaculation as testosterone levels peak around the seventh day. Everyone's experience of this passion cycle is slightly different depending on certain variables such as an individual's sensitivity to certain neurochemicals, whether or not loving affection or a partner are present and the type of sex performed.

During the dopamine lows of the passion cycle we may feel rejected, abandoned or begin to resent our partner or lover as if they are expecting things from us in ways we don't want and we come to love and hate them periodically. We become emotionally attached to the things that simultaneously ease the pain and give us pleasure. What we may have hoped to have been a romantic affair may feel more like a stormy ride at times due to this cycle of attraction and repulsion and its highs and lows.

The orgasm is the glue that creates our addictive outlook on life and makes us dependent on others. We rely on others to make us feel good and special because without them we feel bad and incomplete and as a result we start to resent them. We love them for the way they make us feel but hate them for the fact they can hurt us and that our sense of worth and self-image are dependent on them.

Studies have shown that enkephalins are released during and after an orgasm and this increase in endogenous opioids occurs after one or several ejaculations. Semen has been shown to have antidepressant properties as it contains high levels of melatonin, adrenaline, testosterone, oxytocin, vasopressin, opioids and noradrenaline, all of which affect memory, mood and cognition in a positive way. Researchers have found that women who don't use condoms during sex have lower rates of depression than those who do use condoms as the neurochemicals in semen are absorbed by the body.

The brain becomes less responsive to testosterone after every orgasm as it becomes desensitised and with each orgasm androgen (testosterone) receptor activity drops affecting libido, mood and dopamine levels. Exogenous opiates also affect sexual performance and have been linked to sexual impotence. Opioids inhibit oxytocin production, the *'love chemical'* or *'bonding hormone'* that is released during touch, warmth and sensation. Oxytocin levels rise after climax which causes a rise in prolactin.

Phenylethylamine (PEA) like oxytocin produces feelings of euphoria, attraction and excitement. When we are sexually excited or lustful, the brain releases PEA and levels plateau during an orgasm. When PEA levels increase, dopamine levels rise as dopamine is blocked from being deactivated which leads to dopamine desensitisation and the need to push the envelope to seek out new dopamine highs.

Serotonin is involved in sexual satiation and has been shown to inhibit the dopamine reward pathways. Serotonin and thyrotropin-releasing hormone (TRH) increase the amount of prolactin released by the pituitary gland.

Testosterone and oestrogen are implicated in sexual desire and testosterone levels are higher in men than in women, while oestrogen levels are higher in women than in men. Increased levels of prolactin decrease testosterone in men and oestrogen in women, while decreases in testosterone have been shown to reduce sexual desire in men and decreases in oestrogen have the same effect on women. During sexual excitement and arousal, glutamate levels rise and peak during ejaculation followed by a dip. Vasopressin increases sexual arousal in men but has the opposite effect on women when levels get too high.

Feelings of love, tenderness and sexual satisfaction activate the parasympathetic nervous system which works in opposition to the emotions of up-regulatory arousal that are involved in the *'fight-or-flight'* or *'excite-or-approach'* responses.

Perception & Modality

It is from the act of sex that the lower mind (the animal self/ego) comes into being as sex polarises the soul and as a result we are forever at the whims of the forces of nature until balance is restored. The neurochemical roller-coaster that happens after the orgasm sets off the cycle of emotional unrest and addiction until enlightenment is achieved.

When we are in the lower mind, we consciously identify with the objective sensed universe of motion as a result of the internal chemical imbalance caused by the orgasm and its effect upon our consciousness. We don't see the world as it is but as we are and it is from our emotions that we learn how to be in the world. We become automated parts of this machine universe conditioned by our senses and society.

We go through a series of emotional ups and downs forever seeking balance but never finding it as the emotional pendulum swings back and forth on the wheel of samsara. From birth to death, we are subject to the cycles of life and death until the soul is made whole again.

It is through the act of ejaculatory orgasmic sex that we create a chemical imbalance within that forever seeks rest but only temporarily finds it. This motion is played out through the opposing emotions and their effect upon our neurochemistry and nervous system. This internal imbalance causes a strain on our mind and body through the excess of feel-good chemicals released during an orgasm followed by a dip. These neurochemical ups and downs set in motion the cycles of addiction and emotion.

It is through an impaired nervous system that we lose energy in much the same way that an electrical system that is not properly insulated loses power. When the soul is polarised, we sequentially and periodically give and receive energy that could otherwise have sustained us. One of the main reasons why we have a short life span is because we have forgotten how to retain our sexual energy/life force to extend our lives. Each time we emote we give away part of our soul.

"For what shall it profit a man, if he shall gain the whole world, and lose his own soul?" - Mark 8:36

Input emotions such as fear, pain, love and excitement are the emotions that receive the electrical energies of others, while the output emotions such as anger, desire, happiness and sadness are the output emotions in which we give away the energy that is inherent within us.

When we give away our life force/sexual energy, it has the power to imbue qualities upon the object that we have emoted toward for example, when we find someone attractive and lust after them, we focus and emote our energies toward them. Like a talisman, the person we find attractive will be imbued with an energy that others will pick up on, thinking it was their own thoughts and feelings that the person was attractive but it could have been someone else's thoughts and feelings prior to them that had imbued the person with that energy and attractive quality.

The talismanic power of emotion is particularly evident with the output emotions and imparts particular qualities on the person, dependent on the type of emotion expressed. The quality of the energies imparted, depend largely on the emotion expressed, for example, anger imparts an unattractive quality on a person while lust or desire imparts an attractive quality. Anger imparts negative traits while desire puts a person on a pedestal as they are perceived to have special meaning and that they matter.

Research by Dr Emoto has demonstrated that emotions can physically change the structure of water. Dr Emoto found that positive emotions and prayers affect the structure of water positively and contrastingly negative thoughts and feelings affected the molecular structure of water negatively. The positive effects of prayer and intention upon water created ordered and aesthetically pleasing structures while negative emotions such as hate and pain resulted in disfigured and unpleasant molecular formations.

When we polarise the soul through the orgasm, we place a condition upon the psyche to seek the polarity which it is lacking. Attraction to the other or same sex demonstrates this fact as the other sex represents the polarity that one is lacking internally and as a result we long for unity and to be whole again. When we are aroused by the opposite or same sex, we become sexually excited by an aspect of ourselves that we lack that we see in others which leads to attraction and attachment.

We incorporate into our psyche that which we identify with and are emotionally attached to. We integrate that part of ourselves that we have lost through the act of sex and as a result seek union with it in the material objects that are energetically or chemically polarised and mirror that part of ourselves that we have lost and are lacking. This identification with the external sensed universe and its ever-changing conditions is why we suffer. The cause of this identification with sensation and feeling is an effect of the orgasm upon the psyche.

Chemically and energetically, we unbalance ourselves through the act of sex and seek comfort and pleasure in the objects that elicit sensed and emotional feelings within us. It is not the objects themselves that we become attached to but the feelings derived from them and as a result we self-medicate in an attempt to correct the chemical imbalance within and return to homeostasis.

Sex is natures built-in addiction mechanism that ensures members of the opposite sex seek each other out for the purpose of procreation. It is through the addictive nature of the brain that mating partners become dependent on one another long enough to rear the next generation to ensure the survival of the species.

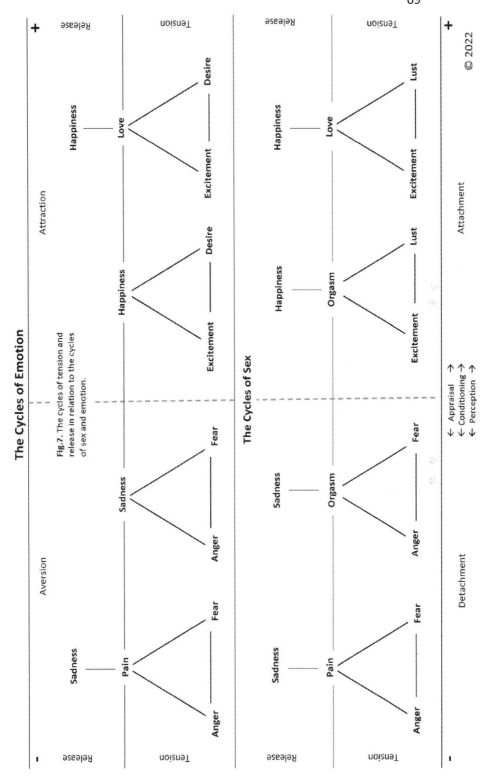

The Cycles of Emotion

Fig.7. The cycles of tension and release in relation to the cycles of sex and emotion.

The Cycles of Sex

© 2022

← Appraisal →
← Conditioning →
← Perception →

Attraction

Aversion

Attachment

Detachment

Release

Tension

Release

Tension

Release

Tension

Release

Tension

Desire — Love — Happiness
Excitement

Happiness — Desire
Excitement

Lust — Love — Happiness
Excitement

Happiness — Orgasm — Lust
Excitement

Sadness — Sadness — Fear
Anger

Sadness — Pain — Fear
Anger

Sadness — Orgasm — Fear
Anger

Sadness — Pain — Fear
Anger

+

+

−

−

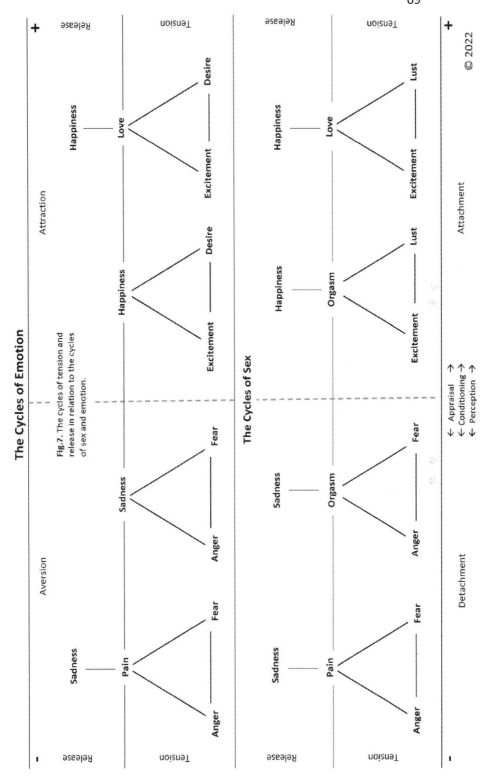

Chapter 8

Love

Love is a contact emotion that connects us to others and drives us to seek union with that which we identify with and mirrors who we are as a whole. Love is nature's way of storing energy into mass and is universal.

In the classical sense, love is a positive emotion relating to touch and is the motive behind sensed pleasures and comfort. Love is an input emotion of down-regulatory arousal that promotes growth and rest and leads to happiness. Happiness is secondary to love.

There are two types of love that relate to the two truths of Buddhism: absolute and relative. Relative love is conditional and absolute love is unconditional. Conditional love is as it implies and is based on sensed and societal conditioning. This type of love is relative to our conditioning and in Buddhism is known as *'attachment'*.

Attachment is related to the sensed universe of motion (feeling) and our identification with it and is characterised by an affection, affiliation and connection to anything that brings a sense of identity, worth, value, completeness, comfort and gain.

Unconditional love is of a higher order and nature than conditional love as unconditional love is absolute and the source of all creation. Unconditional love is the divine love that we experience during a spiritual awakening and is our true essence.

Love is part of the rest-and-digest and tend-and-befriend responses that entail parasympathetic arousal and works in opposition to the fight-or-flight and the excite-or-approach responses that cause us to take action. We appraise the experience and sensation of love as a pleasurable feeling and in its many guises love helps us build interpersonal relationships.

With love we integrate that which we see in a positive light to reap the rewards. We make the other part of who we are as the sense of who we are and positive self-image come from love. We feel whole, complete and confident with love and that everything is right with the world. We do not question the status quo and accept and believe that all is well because we are feeling well. When we are in love, we feel on top of the world, like we matter and that our existence counts. We feel like we have a purpose in life. To the psyche love represents truth, creation, unity, life and light.

Love and pain are two sides of the same coin as they are of the same whole. Love is the positive invert of pain and pain is the negative invert of love as the polarity and effect is in the opposite direction. To love is to become one, to be made whole. Love is the integration of another into the self and pain is the disintegration of another from the self.

Love and pain share similar neural circuitry for facial expression, physiological effects on the body and arousal but are appraised differently due to the differences in neurochemistry, neural activity and experience. Some of the physiological effects of love are the same as pain but appraised positively. The positive traits that accompany love may be due to the release of oxytocin and other feel-good neurochemicals such as gamma-aminobutyric acid, dopamine, phenylethylamine and serotonin that inhibit negative emotions and are implicated in positive appraisal.

The phlegmatic temperament is associated with love. People with this temperament tend to be peaceful, caring and relaxed and are tolerant of others. They are content with themselves, thoughtful and often seek tranquillity.

Neurochemistry & Physiology

The experience of love can be separated into three distinct phases according to Helen Fisher; a leading expert on the subject. Fisher found that each stage of love comes with its own neural circuitry, neurochemistry and behavioural patterns that relate to the cycle of positive emotions.

Lust is the first stage of sexual arousal that entails the increased release of the *'love chemical'* or *'excitant amine'* phenylethylamine (PEA) and the sex hormones oestrogen and testosterone. This phase lasts no longer than a couple of weeks or months and is characterised by feelings of sexual excitement.

Attraction is the second stage of falling in love and is the romantic desire for a mating partner that grows out of lust and is mediated by the arousal and reward neurochemicals PEA, cortisol, dopamine, glutamate, noradrenaline and serotonin.

The attraction stage lasts from one and a half to three years and is characterised by an increase in energy and focused attention on the object of affection, intrusive thoughts and a longing for union with a potential mate or mating partner.

PEA is associated with feelings of excitement, elation, attraction and sexual arousal and causes the release of dopamine and noradrenaline. Studies have shown that the ventral tegmental area (VTA) and caudate nucleus are active during the attraction stage of falling in love and are part of the brain's reward systems that are rich in dopamine. The VTA is implicated in arousal, attention, pleasure and the incentive to seek and obtain rewards. The caudate nucleus is involved in expectation and reward detection, the integration of sensory information and the representation of personal goals.

Noradrenaline is implicated in attraction as it produces characteristics of human romantic love such as increased attention, alertness, appetite loss, energy, sleeplessness and increased memory for new desires. Low levels of serotonin are also associated with the attraction stage and might explain why when we fall in love, our new love interests are constantly on our mind due to serotonin being low when we are not with them. The effects of serotonin on the brain when we fall in love has a similar neurological pattern to that of obsessive-compulsive disorder (OCD) and some suggest that taking anti-depressants such as selective serotonin reuptake inhibitors (SSRIs) and other medications that treat OCD hinder our capacity to fall in love.

Attachment is the last stage of falling in love that promotes bonding and relationships. This stage usually lasts for a number of years and has been linked to higher levels of vasopressin and oxytocin. Attachment is normally based on child-rearing, marriage and common interests and is characterised by feelings of comfort, calmness and oneness.

Love and tender feelings activate the parasympathetic nervous system and promote growth and regeneration. Researchers have found that there are high levels of the protein molecule *'nerve growth factor'* (NGF) when we initially fall in love but these levels return to normal after a year. This initial spurt of growth aids the formation of new neural networks and pathways. It ensures the integration of information into the psyche and that long-term commitments are established.

The long-term effects of attachment are due to the *'cuddle hormone'* oxytocin. Oxytocin helps encourage bonding and forms social networks and has been linked to many functions such as penile erection, pregnancy, maternal instincts and behaviour, uterine contraction, milk release, ejaculation and the orgasm. Oxytocin is released by touch and warmth and regulates the stress response by reducing blood pressure and cortisol levels. Oxytocin promotes positive social interactions such as the tend-and-befriend response. Studies suggest that oxytocin helps us maintain healthy psychological boundaries, boosts positive self-image and regulates our emotional experiences when in close relationships.

Vasopressin plays a role in the long-term commitment stage and like oxytocin is implicated in the mediation of sexual behaviour. Endorphins also regulate sexual behaviour, attachment, pleasure, comfort, stress and pain and some believe that the endorphins released in the attachment phase are the cause of our attachments to others. After the honeymoon period our brains develop a tolerance to PEA and endorphins are released instead. Endorphins enable us to feel relaxed, safe, peaceful and stable over time. This neurochemical shift usually happens within eighteen months to four years into a relationship.

Researchers have found that the insula cortex, anterior cingulate cortex (ACC), caudate nucleus and putamen were active when love-struck volunteers were shown photographs of their loved one and that seeing a lover caused activity in these brain regions that were not activate when a volunteer looked at pictures of a friend. The insula cortex and ACC are involved in gut feelings and homeostatic feedback.

The insula cortex is of particular importance when it comes to love as it plays a role in various functions associated with emotion and homeostasis such as motor control, self-awareness, interpersonal experiences, cognition and perception. Studies have shown that the insula cortex is implicated in emotional processing, anxiety, norm violations, empathy, trust, orgasms and the experience of bodily self-awareness. The insular cortex is where the experience of pain and its intensity is registered and where we imagine pain when looking at images of painful events after thinking about them happening to ourselves.

Some psychologists believe that our emotional experiences and feelings are based on our brain's interpretation of bodily states that are aroused by emotionally charged situations and refer to this phenomenon as *'embodied cognition'*. The insular cortex is where non-painful warmth or non-painful coldness of touch is judged to its degree. Brain images have shown that the insular cortex is active when people experience physical or psychological warmth. The brain cannot tell the difference between social and physical warmth and reacts the same way to both as the neural circuitry for love overlaps that of warmth through physical touch. Based on this evidence, some psychologists believe that our brains evolved to handle complex emotions from the bottom-up and that there was no need for new neural circuitry as the emotional pathways of the brain were built onto the circuits that process basic sensory information.

Perception & Modality

To love is to integrate into one's self, to make part of who we are mentally, physically and emotionally. To love is to become one, to be whole again. With love we integrate that which we see in a positive light to reap the rewards. We make the other part of who we are as the sense of who we are and positive self-image come from love.

When we are in love, we feel whole, complete and confident and that everything is right with the world. We do not question the status quo and accept and believe that all is well because we are feeling well.

When we are faced with situations and the behaviour of others in life, the integration of energy and information is quite simple, we either reject the information or accept it. When we behave in a certain manner, it is because we have picked the behaviour up from others and have been conditioned to reflect that which we identify with. If our parents for example, smoke we are either going to smoke or not smoke depending on social and genetic factors that determine our polarity and preference toward smoking.

The integration of information is how we deal with the facts of life and it operates on an OR mechanism and is very dualistic in nature. We do or we do not accept the behaviour of others and if we break down all learned behaviour, this dualistic principle is behind what behaviour we learn and use in our everyday lives.

In our actions lie statements of what is and what isn't acceptable and these statements in turn give us information about the world and how to live in it and it is from these statements that we deduce the behaviour that is expected from us via friends, family and social groups. These statements are indicators of our values and where they belong in terms of our hierarchy of needs and which personal addictions take priority.

The integration of information and behaviour is partly where our cultural identity comes from and is the logic behind *'taking things at face value'* and *'what you see is what you get'*. With love we accept and integrate the energy and information into the psyche and with pain we reject and disintegrate energy and information from the psyche.

Love is the poison and the antidote. It is not the object of affection that we become attached to, but the feeling and sense of self derived from it. It is only those that we are emotionally attached to that have the power to hurt us emotionally. We become dependent on others and self-medicate in an attempt to address the chemical imbalance within and return to homeostasis. Love and the comfort it brings becomes a temporary solution to the negative emotions and self-doubt we experience when we are low in certain neurochemicals and hormones.

Love is earned through years of sensed and societal conditioning and we become dependent on the things that gave love as they have become an integral part of our psychological make-up and sense of self. Positive self-image and high self-esteem come from years of positive reinforcement and high social standing.

Our sense of self and worth comes from the things that give love such as food, friends, family, hobbies and habits. This conditioned idea of the self is however, only circumstantial and when one falls out of love the illusion is shattered only to find pain. If our parents, loved ones or interests we are passionate about come under attack, our ego perceives it as a threat and acts accordingly. We feel hurt by an attack because we have integrated into the psyche that aspect of ourselves that we have given away and are emotionally attached to.

The relationships that we have with our parents reflect the relationships that we have with the divine and influence our preferences toward sexual partners and lovers. When our ideals of family life and perfection are broken heartache follows. A person's gender identity and preferences are a direct reflection of their relationship to their parents for example, if a child has been emotionally scarred by their father, they may reject the masculine aspect of their personality in favour of the feminine and identify with such.

Our parents reflect the higher aspects of ourselves and as a whole represent perfection. This dynamic toward the masculine and feminine influences our sexual orientation and bias toward which gender we favour and this is how we develop our relationship to the divine and why we often take sides when it comes to family disputes, loving one while hating the other.

Who we are in essence is love, light and energy. This energy can be divided, or it can be whole. When divided we bring into being two unbalanced conditions that forever repeat themselves as conditions of (e) motion. With each emotion that we experience, we become an altered state of consciousness that acts in accordance to the polarity that we have been conditioned into by the senses and society.

We are a machine part in this electric universe of opposed lights while under the influence of the chemistry of emotion and react to external forces that represent aspects of our psyche. The love that we experience in life simulates true love and completes us but only for the moment in which the conditions are right.

The Pairing and Polarity of Emotion with regards to Classification and Type

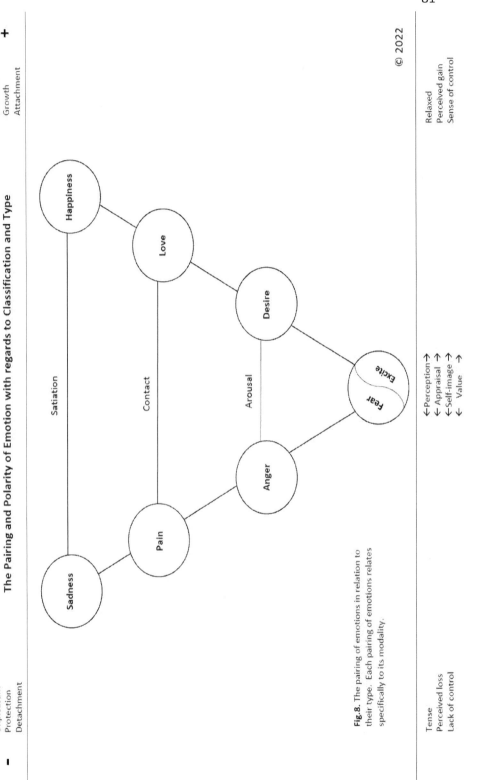

Unpleasant
Protection
Detachment

Pleasant
Growth
Attachment

−   +

Satiation

Contact

Arousal

Happiness

Love

Desire

Fear

Excite

Anger

Pain

Sadness

Fig.8. The pairing of emotions in relation to their type. Each pairing of emotions relates specifically to its modality.

© 2022

← Perception →
← Appraisal →
← Self-image →
← Value →

Tense
Perceived loss
Lack of control

Relaxed
Perceived gain
Sense of control

Chapter 9

Pain

Emotional pain is the unwanted intrusion into the self
which motivates us to withdraw from damaging or
potentially damaging stimuli and situations to protect
the ego and sense of self from harm or loss.

Pain is the feeling we experience when our ability to resist
an unwanted pressure or force is exceeded. Pain is a contact
emotion relating to touch that arises through sensed and
societal conditioning. The first port of call for the ego when
we are in pain is to resist the perceived threat through either
fear or anger unless we are in a safe place to process the
pain or we are already mentally or physically run down.

When we feel hurt, we withdraw and retaliate to find a safe
place to recover and heal our wounds. Pain is part of feeling
neglected or rejected, where we feel deprived and unloved.
In Hans Selye's GAS response to stress, pain occurs in the
exhaustion stage as our efforts to resist a perceived threat
or loss have failed as a result of loss of control, identity and
homeostasis.

Pain is a negative emotion in the classical sense and is
the motivating force behind the fight-or-flight response.
It is one half of the pleasure/pain principle that conditions
us to avoid harmful stimuli. When we are emotionally
hurt, we appraise the situation or sensation negatively,
as the chemistry that accompanies pain is unpleasant
and uncomfortable.

Love and pain are two sides of the same coin as they are of the same whole. Pain is the negative invert of love and love is the positive invert of pain as the polarity and effect of each emotion is in the opposite direction. Pain is the disintegration of information and energy from the psyche, while love is the integration of energy and information into the psyche.

Love causes an overabundance of feel-good chemicals that is followed by an under abundance which we experience as pain. As we experience this under abundance of feel-good chemicals, an excess of feel-bad chemicals flood the brain resulting in what we call *'emotional pain'*.

The opiates to emotional pain are the same neurochemicals involved in positive emotion and in an attempt to address the balance we self-medicate. The comfort of others or substances that elicit a feeling within us act as the antidote to our self-created pain and it is from our emotional attachments to others that pain is born.

Love and pain share similar neural circuitry for facial expression, physiological effects on the body and arousal but are appraised differently due to the differences in neurochemistry, neural activity and experience. Some of the physiological effects of pain are the same as love but appraised negatively. The negative traits that accompany pain are due to the lack of feel-good chemicals such as oxytocin, serotonin and endorphins that inhibit negative emotions and are involved in positive appraisal.

Pain is an input emotion of up-regulatory arousal that motivates the fight-or-flight response and leads to sadness. Sadness is secondary to pain as pain is the signal of loss of homeostasis and sadness is the recognition of that pain or loss.

To the psyche pain represents death, destruction, coldness, darkness, evil, incompleteness, non-existence, separation, decay and imperfection. Pain is part of the grieving process we go through when we have lost something that we are emotionally attached to. Guilt, shame and loneliness are all micro emotions of emotional pain. In mythology this energy goes by the name of Satan, Saturn, Cronos, Shiva, Ahriman and the grim reaper and its primary purpose is to release energy from matter.

Neurochemistry & Physiology

Pain entails the activation of the sympathetic nervous system and works in opposition to the rest-and-digest and tend-and befriend responses that entail parasympathetic arousal. Researchers have found that emotional pain and physical pain share some of the same neural circuitry and mechanisms of action. Studies have shown that the anterior cingulate cortex (ACC), anterior insula cortex and prefrontal cortex are active when the brain feels unpleasantness from experimentally induced emotional or physical pain.

Other areas that are active when the brain experiences emotional pain include the cerebellum, amygdala, thalamus, basal ganglia, posterior cingulate cortex, prefrontal cortex, periaqueductal gray, parahippocampal gyrus and the somatosensory cortices. Based on these findings, some psychologists have proposed in the Social Pain Overlap

Theory (SPOT) that the brain cannot tell the difference between physical and emotional pain and reacts the same way to both. The neural circuitry for emotional pain is piggybacked onto the same neural circuitry that handles basic sense perceptions and as a result we identify with the objective universe of sensed motion and feeling.

The brain treats physical and emotional pain the same way and this is why we treat both types of pain with substances or stimuli that elicit a positive emotional response within us. The neurochemicals involved in the modulation of physical pain are the same neurochemicals involved in emotional pain. Some of the neurochemicals involved in the experience of pain include adenosine triphosphate, neuropeptide Y, glutamate, calcitonin gene-related peptide, vasoactive intestinal polypeptide, somatostatin, bombesin, bradykinin, neurokinin A and B, nitrous oxide and substance P.

Research indicates that the neural networks for love and pain overlap and that love acts as a modulator of physical and emotional pain. The opioid and dopamine systems have been shown to have an impact on our experience of pain. The main neurotransmitters involved in the modulation and inhibition of pain include endorphins, enkephalins, dynorphins, dopamine, serotonin, noradrenaline, gamma-aminobutyric acid, neurotensin, acetylcholine, cannabinoids and oxytocin. Studies have shown that the opioid system is involved in relieving emotional pain in the form of separation and distress and oxytocin the *'cuddle hormone'* has been found to modulate pain when administered to test subjects exogenously.

Perception & Modality

The function of pain and what it represents to the psyche is to liberate energy from matter as pain is the disintegrating principle of nature where the disintegration of another from the self occurs. When we are in pain, we feel separated, detached, disconnected, incomplete and worthless. We feel that something is missing in life and self-medicate to fill the void within us.

When we are hurt, we feel unloved and rejected and that our lives are meaningless. We see the world through a negative filter and have a bleak outlook on life. We question who we are as our sense of self is brought into question and we doubt our worth. We question our abilities and confidence to look after ourselves and often think we are bad people because we feel bad.

Our sense of self and self-worth are born out of our emotional attachments to others and when something questions our worth and/or our sense of self and confidence, we feel hurt. When people attack that which we are emotionally attached to, we perceive it as an attack on ourselves because we have integrated them into our psyche and they have become part of who we are. It is only those that we are emotionally attached to and have become part of our psychological makeup that have the power to hurt us.

Pain is full of cognitive distortions as we see the glass as being half-empty and ask, *'what have I done to deserve this?'* We see the world in terms of potential enemies and not allies and we become cynical of the world and all that is in it. We lose faith in life and in people and feel justified in our destructive behaviours. Statements like *'no one gives a damn so why should I'* or *'it was only a matter of time, so I attacked first'* are all born out of pain and the cynicism that accompanies it. We question everything and trust no one when we are hurt and believe everyone is out to get us and look for someone to blame. We blame ourselves and/or others for the perceived social injustices that caused us to feel pain.

Victim mentality and negativity are characteristics of pain. We see the world in a very detached way and think the world is against us. We see ourselves and the environment we live in, in a negative light and we constantly search our surroundings and environment for potential threats. We look for errors and imperfections and only see the differences in people and not the similarities. We think, feel and act in terms of separating that which we see as a threat.

Escapism is born out of pain and our aversion to it. When we don't feel right, we often use that which we are emotionally attached to, to escape the unpleasant feeling. The comfort of activities or things that elicit a feeling within us act as the antidote to our self-created pain.

Chapter 10

Sadness

Sadness is an emotional response to loss and detachment from that which we are emotionally attached to that is characterised by feelings of disappointment, separation, loss and helplessness.

In Hans Selye's Gas response to stress sadness occurs in the exhaustion stage. When our efforts to resist an external stressor fail we experience this as a loss to the sense of self and homeostasis. Depression and burnout are part of the exhaustion stage when the stressor has become too much to bear.

Sadness is a satiation emotion relating to contentment or lack of and is the release half of the tension-release cycle of emotion that leads to rest so we can prepare ourselves for new challenges ahead. Sadness is an output emotion of down-regulatory arousal that helps release the build-up of neurotoxins in the body that have accumulated from the negative emotions of up-regulatory arousal.

We are often quiet, withdrawn and lethargic when we are sad and when our emotional and physical needs are not met or are taken from us, we feel sad. The loss of basic needs such as food, clothing and shelter makes us feel sad as does the loss of what we are emotionally attached to.

The brain treats sadness and pain alike as pain is the signal of loss of homeostasis and sadness is the recognition of that pain or loss. In the classical sense, sadness is a negative emotion of down-regulation that helps us dissolve the neurochemicals involved in the negative emotions of up-regulatory arousal and encourages rest.

Sadness is part of the grieving process and when we are sad, we cry. The tears and comfort that sadness brings dissolves fear and anger as the neurochemicals involved in sadness down-regulate the negative emotions of up-regulatory arousal.

Happiness and sadness are two sides of the same coin as they are of the same whole. Sadness is the negative invert of happiness and happiness is the positive invert of sadness as the polarity and effect of each emotion is in the opposite direction. Sadness is the recognition of a loss and happiness is the recognition of a gain.

Happiness and sadness share similar neural circuitry for facial expression, physiological effects on the body and arousal but are appraised differently due to differences in neurochemistry, neural activity and experience. Some of the physiological effects of sadness are the same as happiness but appraised negatively. The negative traits that accompany sadness may be due to the lack of feel-good chemicals such as serotonin, oxytocin and endorphins that inhibit negative emotions and are implicated in positive appraisal.

Sadness drains us of energy as it disintegrates and separates that which was once part of who we are on a chemical, mental and energetic level. The disintegration of another from the self occurs through the process of letting go where we say our goodbyes once and for all to the person, place or object that we were emotionally attached to. Sadness is a natural part of feeling neglected and rejected where we feel deprived, hurt and at a loss. Grief, depression, melancholy and dysphoria are some of the mood disorders related to sadness.

The melancholic temperament is associated with people who are easily saddened. People with the melancholic temperament tend to be cautious, serious and introverted and see themselves and the world in a negative light.

Neurochemistry & Physiology

Sadness works predominantly on the parasympathetic nervous system and promotes rest as opposed to the sympathetic nervous system that is implicated in up-regulatory arousal. When we are sad, we fall asleep easily as sadness slows down our heart rate, breathing rate and blood pressure. There are also increases in finger temperature and skin conductance.

Some of the physiological effects of sadness include a fullness behind the eyes and in the throat, a heaviness of chest and limbs and a heightened sensitivity to pain. Sadness uses the same mechanisms of expression as happiness however, the chemistry involved in sadness has a different effect on the muscles affected and has an inverse effect to that of happiness. When we are sad the face drops, the eyes focus downward, the nose wrinkles and the lips quiver. Tears and the feeling that we are about to cry are signs of sadness.

Studies show that the neurotransmitter systems that modulate attachment are involved in sadness. Sadness is associated with low levels of dopamine, noradrenaline, serotonin, oxytocin and endorphins. Endorphin levels have been found to decrease when we are sad and increase when we are around an attachment figure. Oxytocin levels decrease when we are sad and increase after touching, imagining or being with someone we love. Researchers have found that memory-induced sadness reduces oxytocin levels in females and that low levels of oxytocin are associated with depression and separation anxiety.

High levels of dynorphin, corticotrophin releasing factor, monoamine oxidase, substance P and peptide neuro-transmitters are involved in sadness. Increases in dynorphin make us feel sad and have been found to be involved in addiction, analgesia, appetite, circadian rhythms, depression and stress.

Studies have shown that crying reduces stress and the negative physiological effects that are associated with negative emotions. Researchers have discovered that crying releases toxins from the body and that the tears of joy have a different chemical profile than the tears of sadness. Tears caused by emotion have been found to contain leucine enkaphalin, prolactin, adrenocorticotropic hormone, water, minerals and serotonin.

Psychologists have discovered that low levels of serotonin are associated with crying episodes and that a single dose of a selective serotonin reuptake inhibitor antidepressant can reduce the sobbing of healthy women and the sobbing of people who suffer from crying too much. Studies have also found that the emotional tears from women down-regulate aggressive behaviour in men and halts their sex drive.

Sadness generates activity in over 70 regions of the brain in none depressed volunteers. Some of the regions that are involved in sadness include the insula cortex, anterior and posterior cingulate cortex, ventrolateral prefrontal cortex, lateral prefrontal cortex, dorsolateral prefrontal cortex, superior and middle temporal gyrus, the cerebellum and basal ganglia.

Imaging studies of people with major depression have found that depression and sadness share some of the same neural territory as some of the regions of the brain that are implicated in sadness overlap with areas that are known to be hyperactive or hypoactive in people with major depression. There is greater activity in the right prefrontal cortex and less activity in the left prefrontal cortex. The right prefrontal cortex searches for something novel to snap us out of sadness and into hope and happiness as it looks for changes in the environment and alerts us to novelty.

Perception & Modality

Sadness starts with the acknowledgement of loss of an object, goal, person, place or positively appraised aspect of the self that we are emotionally attached to. For someone to perceive something as a loss, that something must have brought them comfort or arousal in some shape or form for it to elicit the sadness response within them.

When we are sad, our attention focuses inwardly on memories and thoughts of what we have lost. Our thinking becomes ruminative and a tendency towards perceiving our own helplessness is common as sadness shuts down our interest in pleasurable things. The retrieval and encoding of memories and the recognition of cause and effect intensify with sadness as the brain retrieves only sad memories.

Sadness slows down the cognitive and motor functions so that we can reflect deeper, look for the source of concern and contemplate the perceived failure or disappointment. Our perception of time slows down and our reality is distorted when we are sad as everything seems dark, cold and lifeless. Feelings of emptiness and despair are part of feeling sad.

We respond to sadness either by facing our loss or by avoiding it. Perceptually sadness is quite dumb as it motivates us to seek the nearest thing to us to relieve it. We reach for the things that bring comfort, often in the form of sensed pleasures to avert ourselves from the unpleasantness of sadness.

The fight-or-flight response is motivated by sadness and pain as anger and fear act as defence mechanisms to harm/loss. In the short-term fear and anger protect us/the ego from harm/loss but in the long run they damage the body as the brain masks the effects of stress via the release of endorphins. Anger drains us of endorphins, adrenaline and noradrenaline and when the body is low in these feel-good neurochemicals, we feel sad.

Sadness slows us down and encourages rest, it gives us time to recover after a bout of anger. Self-hatred and low self-esteem often accompany sadness as we accept the perceived loss of control, loss of homeostasis and loss of sense of self. A sense of unfairness and yearning often accompany sadness and the bitter-sweet realisation of our loss.

When we experience a major loss in life, we go through the grieving process where we let go, disintegrate and get ready for the new challenges ahead. Initially, we may express our loss through tears as tears express our sorrow and distress to others. The expressions *'a cry for help'* and *'a good cry'* are often used to refer to the tears that bring help and the comfort of others. Crying however, can create discomfort in others when we don't know how to help someone who is upset.

The tears of loved ones or friends can distress us at times because there is a cry for help that we do not know how to give and when we don't know how to help someone who is sad, we begin to question our worth as our worth is relative to others. The sadness of others can induce feelings of guilt and make us feel bad about ourselves because of our perceived failures. When we are sad, we sometimes seek somewhere private to cry so we don't have to ask others for help. We find solitude in isolation to hide the tears that could attract guilt-induced sympathy from others.

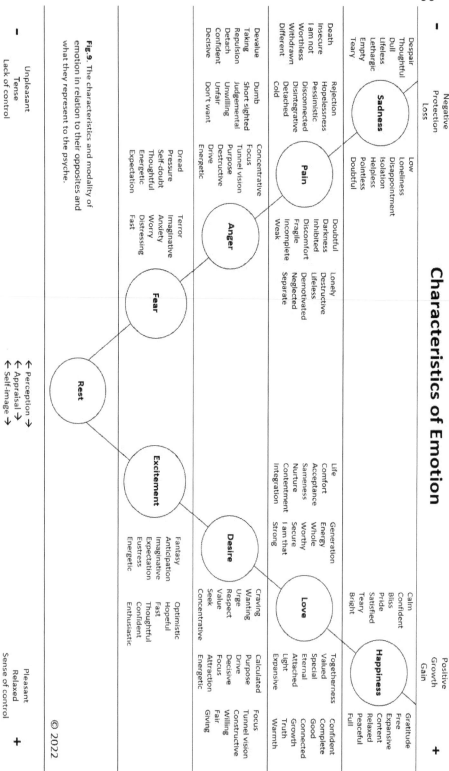

Characteristics of Emotion

Negative
Protection
Loss

Positive
Growth
Gain

Fig. 9. The characteristics and modality of emotion in relation to their opposites and what they represent to the psyche.

− Unpleasant Tense Lack of control

+ Pleasant Relaxed Sense of control

← Perception →
← Appraisal →
← Self-image →

© 2022

Chapter 11

Happiness

Happiness is an emotional response to a perceived
gain that is characterised by feelings of contentment,
appreciation, satisfaction, gratitude, pleasure and pride.
The destination emotion is a satiation emotion relating to
contentment and is the release half of the tension-release
cycle of emotions in the positive sense.

When our physical and emotional constants are met for
food, clothing, shelter and union with that which we are
emotionally attached to, we feel happy. Happiness is an
output emotion of down-regulatory arousal that regulates
the positive and negative feedback mechanisms of emotion
as happiness is a goal-orientated destination emotion that
allows the body to return to a state of rest for rejuvenation,
or another attempt at repeating the positive experience
again and/or to seek out new endeavours.

Happiness is the positive appraisal of an internal feeling
brought on by pleasure, love, acceptance, freedom and
gain and is the pleasure half of the pleasure/pain principle.
The experience of happiness is the final chemical goal in
the neocortex that is the result of an overabundance of
feel-good chemicals such as serotonin, endorphins and
gamma-aminobutyric acid (GABA).

Happiness is driven by the senses as the things that we
desire are the things that excite us and the things that
excite us are the things that we have been programmed
to like via the senses and society.

When we get what we want there is no need to be aroused while we reap the benefits of our rewards and perceived gains. Happiness is the recognition of the integration of a perceived gain into the self and is part of the rest-and-digest response where we feel satisfied with our gains. It is the recognition that we have gotten what we wanted and that our efforts have paid off.

Sadness and happiness are two sides of the same coin as are of the same whole. Happiness is the positive invert of sadness and sadness is the negative invert of happiness as the polarity and effect of each emotion is in the opposite direction. Happiness is the recognition of a gain and sadness is the recognition of a loss.

Happiness and sadness share similar neural circuitry for facial expression, physiological effects on the body and arousal but are appraised differently due to differences in neurochemistry, neural activity and experience. Some of the physiological effects of happiness are the same as sadness but appraised positively. The positive traits that accompany happiness may be due to the release of endorphins and other feel-good chemicals that are responsible for down-regulating the up-regulatory emotions of arousal and are implicated in positive appraisal.

Neurochemistry & Physiology

Happiness works predominantly on the parasympathetic nervous system as opposed to the sympathetic nervous system that is implicated in up-regulatory arousal. There is no major shift in physiology with happiness which helps the body recover easily from the biological arousal of up-regulatory emotions. The body maintains a state of poise and is at ease as happiness is associated with lower blood pressure, low heart rate, low muscle tension and lower skin conductance.

With happiness the muscles around the corners of the eyes and mouth contract causing them to move upwards creating a smile. A genuine smile triggers a biochemical event that releases the feel-good neurotransmitters dopamine, serotonin and endorphins. If the muscles around the eyes are not stimulated, the neurotransmitters and neural networks are not switched on. The muscles around the eyes have to be moved to bring about the physiology of happiness.

High levels of acetylcholine, endorphins, dopamine, anandamide, noradrenaline, serotonin, gonadotropin releasing hormone, oxytocin, vasopressin, melatonin and GABA are associated with happiness. The feel-good chemicals dopamine and serotonin have been shown to mediate negative thoughts and feelings and are involved in positive emotions and mind states.

Serotonin mediates happiness, optimism and satisfaction and low levels of serotonin have been found in people who are suffering from depression. Low levels of noradrenaline are also associated with depression while high levels have been linked to feelings of euphoria and elation.

High levels of endorphins are involved in happiness and are released during exercise, eating, music, laughter, love and during an orgasm. High concentrations have been shown to inhibit pain, while low levels are linked to negative emotions. Happiness is associated with low levels of adrenaline, substance P, dynorphin, cortisol, corticotropin-releasing factor and adrenocorticotropic hormone.

The brain has a large network of reward circuits that are known as *'rewards pathways'* or *'pleasure centres'* which include the brainstem, nucleus accumbens, ventral pallidum, insular cortex, cingulate cortex, orbitofrontal cortex and medial prefrontal cortex.

A vast amount of emotional processing is done by the prefrontal cortex (PFC) and some psychologists suggest that the PFC may act like a working memory, balancing the approach and withdrawal responses in order to handle our goals and how to accomplish them. Each hemisphere and various sub regions of the PFC specialise in different roles. The left PFC enquires and is implicated in the approach response, it helps us approach things to satisfy our needs and is involved in positive affect. Researchers have found that damage to the front part of the left PFC is associated with depression. The right PFC on the other hand, makes us withdraw from a given situation and is involved in negative affect and damage to the right PFC has been shown to cause manic, expansive reactions in people.

Studies suggest that the orbital prefrontal cortex (OFC) is involved in punishments and rewards, with the right OFC reacting to punishments and the left OFC reacting to rewards. Happiness involves greater activity in the left PFC and studies of Tibetan monks have found that meditation resulted in exceptionally high levels of activity on the left side of the brain. The activity in the monks' left PFC was the highest ever recorded. The PCF has been shown to be implicated in emotional responses and has numerous connections to other parts of the brain that are responsible for controlling dopamine, noradrenaline, serotonin and endorphin levels.

Comparison of some of the physiological effects of happiness and sadness.

Happiness	Sadness
Decreased heart rate	Decreased heart rate
Parasympathetic nervous system activation	Parasympathetic nervous system activation
Decreased blood pressure	Decreased blood pressure
Increased energy	Decreased energy
Decreased sensory alertness	Increased sensory alertness
Left prefrontal cortex activation	Right prefrontal cortex activation
Muscle movement around the eyes or tears	Muscle movement around the eyes or tears
Low skin conductance	High skin conductance
low muscle tension	low muscle tension
Muscle movement around the mouth 😊	Muscle movement around the mouth 🙁

Perception & Modality

Happiness begins with an awareness of a perceived gain
to an attachment figure, goal, object or valued aspect of
the self. For someone to perceive something as a gain,
that something must have brought them comfort or arousal
in some shape or form for it to bring them happiness.

The things that we desire are things that make us feel
good and a sense of worth and gain derive from them. We
come to love the things that make us feel happy and become
emotionally attached to all the things that elicit a chemical
reaction within us. Happiness fosters attachment rather than
detachment as happiness is an effect that accompanies the
awareness that an attachment has been reinforced. It is
secondary to attachment.

Happiness can only be achieved with a certain blend
of feel-good chemicals that quell and inhibit negative
emotions. Happiness is dependent on our perception and
appraisal of the self and/or situation and is often wrong.
We can become happy for the wrong reasons and value the
wrong things. We can be attached to things that are bad for
our health or life but still carry on these negative habits and
patterns of behaviour because they make us feel good and
when we feel good, we think we are good because we
identify with our thoughts and feelings and become them.

When we are happy, we accept the current status quo and
see things in a good light. We don't question things because
we have gotten what we wanted. We go from happiness
to sadness when the things that made us feel good are
no longer available and we have to readjust chemically

from that which created an over-abundance of feel-good chemicals within and let go of the thing that once made us feel good. In the carnal sense, happiness is the antidote to negative emotions as the neural circuitry and neuro-chemistry involved in happiness quells negative thoughts and feelings.

The final goal of all addictions is the release of an over-abundance of feel-good chemicals in the brain that were initially set up through the orgasm or consummatory practices. Addictions such as sex, gambling, overeating, smoking, drinking, drugs and a lust for power and control are all related to and a result of a chemical imbalance within.

Happiness is full of cognitive distortions as we see the world through rose tinted glasses and see the cup as being *'half full'* rather than *'half empty'*. The perception of time and reality is distorted when we are happy as time speeds up and everything seems bright, warm and full of life. Dopamine slows the cognitive and motor systems down creating a sense of speeding time.

When we are happy our attention turns outwardly towards that which we value. We see our perceived gains as being fair and just and think we deserve to reap the rewards because we are worth it. In western cultures we take pride in all that we have accumulated and achieved and integrate the things that we desire into our lives to reap the benefits of the feelings that will derive from them. It is through this sense of achievement and gain that our sense of control and worth are confirmed. We feel special because we have gotten what we wanted.

Our mind is sure that it is a winner when we are happy and it is from our adequacy in getting what we want that we feel special and our sense of self and worth is reinforced. Happiness is associated with high self-esteem and self-love as we accept the perceived gains, sense of importance, sense of self and sense of control. The objects of desire make us feel important, that we matter and that our existence has meaning and purpose. We desire the things that boost our sense of worth and make us feel special. We feel special when we have been discriminated for in the positive sense and are treasured because of what we can offer.

With happiness comes a false sense of confidence and pride. When we get what we want all the time it can be a bad thing. Happiness in the form of pride is one of the seven deadly sins in Christianity. We can experience happiness in cruel, narcissistic and shallow ways. Happiness can be heartless when celebrating in a victory that humiliates or injures others or when we get relief from causing misery to others and we can be arrogant when reveling in the joy of winning as if we are the only ones that matter.

When we get what we want endorphins render the neo-cortex inoperative as we no longer need to think of ways to get the things of value as the destination goal, emotion or feeling has been achieved. Happiness and the comfort it brings is the antidote to sadness and other negative emotions. The energy of happiness radiates from us as a signal of the successful integration of energy into the self.

When we are happy with our perceived gains and newly found or reinforced connections, we give freely of our life force to each other in which we integrate into each other's psyche. This integrative principle is nature's method of storing energy into mass and is how we form bonds.

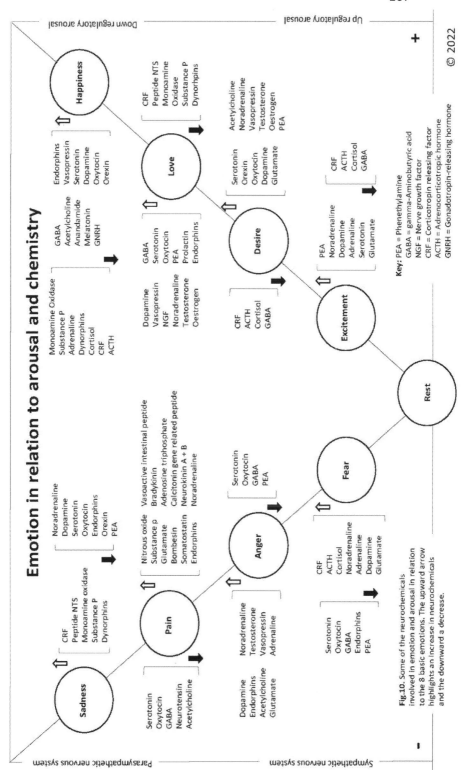

Emotion in relation to arousal and chemistry

Fig.10. Some of the neurochemicals involved in emotion and arousal in relation to the 8 basic emotions. The upward arrow highlights an increase in neurochemicals and the downward a decrease.

Key: PEA = Phenethylamine
GABA = gamma-Aminobutyric acid
NGF = Nerve growth factor
CRF = Corticotropin releasing factor
ACTH = Adrenocorticotropic hormone
GNRH = Gonadotropin-releasing hormone

© 2022

Chapter 12

Enlightenment

Enlightenment is a state of being that has transcended the cycles of carnal emotion, death and karmic rebirth. It is a state of consciousness that is free from sin and suffering. The word Enlightenment means in light in mind (from Greek *en* 'in', cognate with Latin *in,* and *ment* from Latin *mente* meaning mind*).*

Enlightenment is a western term that has been used to describe what the eastern traditions of Buddhism and Hinduism refer to as *'kensho', 'moksha', 'bodhi', 'satori'* or *'nirvana'*. Jesus Christ and Gautama Buddha both taught the path to enlightenment from an eastern and western perspective and founded the saviour religions of the world.

The eastern perspective of enlightenment focuses on the psychological process of awakening in relation to the science of the mind and the western perspective focuses on the physiological process of awakening in relation to the science of the stars and soul when interpreted in the correct manner. Both perspectives have their foundation in astrotheology however, Christianity has a strong emphasis on alchemy, the chemistry of man.

Buddha and Christ are titles given to those who have achieved enlightenment. The word *'Buddha'* means *'the enlightened one'*, *'the knowing one'* or *'the awakened one'*, and *'Christ'* is a Greek translation of the Hebrew word *'Messiah'*, meaning *'the anointed one'*.

Within the mystery schools and occult teachings, enlightenment is sometimes referred to as *'the great work'*,
'ascension' or *'illumination'*. In the western world, spiritual
enlightenment has come to embody the discovery of the
true self or essence that has been masked over by our
sensed and social conditioning.

Religion is the science of the stars and soul told in parables
and prose. The word *'religion'* means *'union'*, *'to connect'*,
'bind' or *'choose'* in its various forms. The holy science is
as old as mankind itself, but overtime has adapted to fit
the celestial clock and our understanding of ourselves
and the universe. All the major religious texts of the world
are guidebooks on how to become enlightened when
interpreted in the correct manner.

Enlightenment is the unification of the masculine and
feminine energies of the psyche, so the soul becomes one
androgynous whole. To become enlightened is to become
chemically and energetically perfected and free from the
addiction of carnal emotions.

When the soul is unified, the polarities of the solar and
lunar energies become one as we become the androgynous
celestial Adam who has realised the Christ within and who
no longer identifies with the sensed universe of motion and
feeling. It is through the unification of opposites within that
the Christ within is born and we free ourselves from our
sensed and societal conditioning.

Neurochemistry and Physiology

Modern science knows very little about the chemistry
and physiology of enlightenment as enlightened people
are a rare commodity as the scientific teachings of old

have been grossly misinterpreted.

In George W. Carey's book, *'God-Man; The Word Made Flesh'* it states that;

"The early Christians knew that the Scriptures, whether written in ancient Hebrew or the Greek, were allegories, parables or fables based on the human body "fearfully and wonderfully made."

The word *'Christ'* comes from the Greek word *christos* meaning *'anointed one'* and the Essenes knew and taught that the Christ within was an oil-like substance created in the body known as the *'Sacred Secretion', 'Christ oil'* or *'Chrism'.*

"This mystery has been kept in the dark for a long time, but now it's out in the open. God wanted everyone, not just Jews, to know this rich and glorious secret inside and out, regardless of their background, regardless of their religious standing. The mystery in a nutshell is just this: Christ is in you, so therefore you can look forward to sharing in God's glory. It's that simple." - Colossians 1, 26:29

The place Calvery or Golgotha where Jesus was crucified translates from the Aramaic and Latin languages to mean *'skull'*. Primitive Christians were aware that the crucifixion was an internal biological process whereby the Christ oil was transformed (to crucify doesn't mean to kill but to increase in power a thousandfold) and returned to the brain to achieve enlightenment (Christ consciousness).

The Claustrum, meaning *'barrier'* or *'cloister'* is located in the centre of the brain and is responsible from the age of twelve (adolescence) for secreting the oil. This oil is described by George W. Carey as *"the source and cause of the physical expression called man"* and the *"River that flows out of Eden (the upper brain) to water the garden."*, the garden symbolising the human body.

Saint Claus or Santa Claus (Claus-trum) is derived from this holy science as the precious fluid descends down the spinal cord (chimney) at Christ-mas, carrying gifts for us (enlightenment) as long as we've done the good work and have been good children.

After being secreted from the claustrum, the oil splits into two parts with one half sent to the pituitary body on the anterior side of the thalamus and the other to the pineal gland on the posterior where they are then differentiated to become a white and a yellow fluid. The Bible refers to these fluids as *'milk and honey'* and is the promise given to the children of Israel to return to this land.

"If the LORD delights in us, he will bring us into this land and give it to us, a land that flows with milk and honey."
- Numbers 14:8

The white milk-like substance created in the pituitary has magnetic properties representing the yin, lunar and feminine energy and is symbolised in the Bible as Mother Mary. The pituitary gland activates the hypothalamus releasing vasopressin and oxytocin which aid health, stimulate the pineal gland and strengthen feelings of compassion, trust and harmony.

The golden yellow, honey-like fluid produced in the pineal gland has electric properties, representing the yang, solar, masculine energies and relates to Joseph in the Bible. The pineal produces melatonin which works as a powerful antioxidant boosting the immune system and suppressing cortisol to reduce stress on the body. It has anti-aging properties and regulates circadian rhythms.

The milk and honey-like oils (Mary and Joseph) travel from the brain down the spinal cord (allegorised by the River of Jordan) via the Ida and Pingala nerve channels to the Sacrum. The Sacral or *'sacred'* Plexus (*'os sacrum'* is Latin meaning sacred) near the base of the spine is allegorised by the *'Dead Sea'* and the point where the spine (River of Jordan) enters it.

The route the oils pass down the spinal cord (River of Jordan) is symbolised biblically by Mary and Joseph's journey to Bethlehem to await the arrival of their spiritual son (the Christ seed). Bethlehem is another name for the solar plexus as it is situated at the pit of the stomach and Bethlehem in Hebrew means *'house of bread'*.

 "I am the living bread that came down from heaven. If anyone eats of this bread, he will live forever. And the bread that I will give for the life of the world is my flesh."
- John 6:51.

The ancients taught that once a month (every twenty-eight and a half days) when the moon is astrologically in the sun sign that you were born in, you receive a psycho-physical germ or Christ seed (unit of chi/Christ energy/life force). This Christ seed is planted within a small cradle shaped depression (manger) in the solar plexus and has an odor of fish which led to the name Jesus (from the Greek word *'Ichtos'* meaning fish).

When the Christ seed (bread of life) arrives in the solar plexus (manger in Bethlehem), it combines with the milk and honey-like secretions (Mary and Joseph) which fertilise the seed and the oil becomes anointed or 'Christed'. This Christ oil was also known as the 'fruit of the Tree of Life'. The Tree of Life represented the vagus nerve and nervous system in which the fruit or seed was carried up the Tree of Life (nervous system) and back to the brain (garden of Eden).

In his book, Carey talks about the 'Tree of good and evil' and saving the seed, stating:

"Good, if saved and "cast upon the waters" (circulation) to reach the Pineal Gland; and evil, if eaten or consumed in sexual expression on the physical plane, or by alcoholic drinks, or gluttony that causes ferment acid and even alcohol in intestinal tract thus "No drunkard can inherit the Kingdom of Heaven" for acids and alcohol cut, or chemically split, the oil that unites with the mineral salts in the body and thus produces the monthly seed".

Eating from the Tree of Good and Evil is seen in the story of Adam and Eve and their fall from grace and the garden of Eden. George W. Carey goes on further stating that:

"The fruit of the Tree of Life, therefore, is the "Fish-bread" of which thou shalt not eat on the plane of animal or Adam (earth- dust of the earth plane): but to "Him that overcometh will I give to eat of the fruit of the Tree of Life," because he saved it and it returned to him in the cerebellum, the home of the Spiritual man, the Ego".

Once anointed, the Christ oil works its way back up the thirty-three vertebrae of the spine to reach the medulla oblongata where the Ida and Pingala nerve channels cross and contact the cerebellum. The Christ oil is then crucified (amplified in power a thousandfold) at the cross (Ida and Pingala nerves) and laid to rest for two and a half days (the length of time the moon stays in each sun sign) just as Jesus was crucified on a cross at thirty-three in Calvary (the skull) and remained in the tomb for two and a half days.

When the Christ oil is saved through righteous living it ascends on the third day to the pineal gland and enlightenment is achieved.

"The Pineal Gland is the "Pinnacle of the Temple." The modus operandi by which the oil of the spinal cord reaches the Pineal Gland is described in what follows:

"There is no name under Heaven whereby ye may be saved except Jesus Christed and then crucified" (correct rendering of the Greek text)." - George W. Carey

The story of Jacobs ladder is also an allegory relating to the science of enlightenment. When Jacob lays his head on the stone (Sacrum) and climbs the ladder (spinal column), he meets God face to face (enlightenment), he called the place he found *'Peniel'* (Pineal):

"So Jacob named the place Peniel, for he said, "I have seen God face to face, yet my life has been preserved." - Genesis 32:30

In modern terms to become enlightened or illumined is to become chemically and energetically (spiritually) perfected and free from the addiction of carnal emotions and orgasmic ejaculatory sex.

When we become enlightened, the feel-good chemicals of the brain such as dopamine, serotonin, oxytocin and endorphins are now at levels that are within the normal ranges for the brain and its related nervous systems to function properly in a balanced manner. The mental obsessions with and the physiological compulsions of others are diminished through the correct balance of neurochemicals within the brain in the regions that are responsible for self-image, awareness and emotion.

It is likely that the anterior cingulate cortex and insula cortex are responsible for the sense of self that we have and our identification with the sensed universe of motion and feeling. These brain regions have been found to be involved in the regulation of heart rate and blood pressure, morality, impulse control, homeostasis, self-awareness, reward anticipation, empathy and emotional pain.

Perception and Modality

When we become enlightened, we become the ideal man, the perfected or complete human being who has realised their true nature. We no longer identify with the sensed universe of motion as our Soul has become one androgynous whole and we have become a holy (whole) person.

An enlightened Soul is the manifestation of the balance between the positive and negative or masculine and feminine energies of the psyche. When our bodies have become chemically perfected, we are no longer subject to the cycles of carnal emotion as we have ascended the Christ oil within and unified the soul. The addictive nature of the carnal mind is eliminated through the process of awakening to the true nature of the self and reality. We no longer think of ourselves as social animals struggling for survival but rather see ourselves as divine beings operating from free will, true love and true joy.

When we have a full awakening and achieve enlightenment, we free ourselves from the addictive nature of the lower mind and the chemistry that kept the cycle in motion. Where there was once the cyclic overabundance of feel-good chemicals in the brain followed by an under abundance, there is now balance. Consciously we have achieved a state of being that is in perfect harmony with itself and is in a state of ease and rest. All nervousness, greed, unrest and irritability are extinguished from our constitution due to the fact that the sympathetic and parasympathetic nervous systems are now in perfect harmony with one another as we are not being overtaxed by the chemistry of emotion.

The electricity that runs through the nervous system is the life force that animates us into action and when the sympathetic and parasympathetic nervous systems are in opposition to one another, this current of energy is lost like a faulty electrical cable that is not properly insulated, but when the sympathetic and parasympathetic nervous systems are in union with each other the life force within illuminates us and fills us with light.

When the body is clean enough and health is restored, we are not moved by peer pressure or the negative energies of others as we have found the immovable spot as mentioned in Buddhism. When enlightened we become very sensitive to the energies others emote but cannot be moved by them. We see the true nature of reality beyond this illusory sensed universe of motion.

The spine is the means by which the emotional energy of others is felt the most as it is the backbone of the central nervous system that animates the whole body. After we have achieved enlightenment however, we can still become sick if we do not look after our bodies and we can still experience emotions but not self-created ones (the emotions that others project towards us) when we have psychoactive substances such as cacao as cacao can open the psyche up and allow the energies of others to enter us.

We can unbalance the nervous system and our neuro-chemistry from without via sensory stressors (animal products, junk food, drugs, medication, toxins, sensations) or from within via the orgasm or too many ejaculations. In epigenetic terms the DNA of our being acts in accordance to our internal chemistry. What we put into our bodies is as equally important as to what we expel from our bodies and can change a genes behaviour with regards to chemical set points.

When we are free from emotion, we perceive the world in a new light, we see things as they are and accept life in its totality. We see that the world is in perfect harmony because we ourselves are in perfect harmony and we come to realise that we are not our bodies but that which animates them as our consciousness has come to know through direct experiential knowledge that we still exist without our thoughts and feelings and we no longer identify with them.

Fig.11. The *'Materia Prima Lapidis Philosophorum,'* is from the *Circle of the Gold and Rosicrucians* (Kirchweger, 1781) and depicts the unification of the masculine and feminine energies of the psyche giving birth to the divine child.

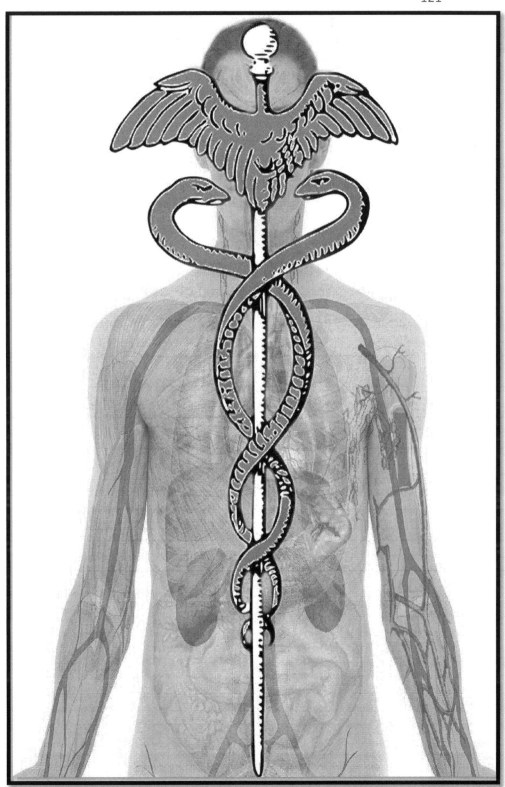

Fig.12. The caduceus has been used for centuries to symbolise the sympathetic and parasympathetic nervous system in relation to spiritual enlightenment. The two snakes intertwined up the staff of Hermes represent the sympathetic and parasympathetic nervous systems.

Final Word

It is through spiritual enlightenment that we can set ourselves free from our sensed and societal conditioning and we can come to know ourselves and God directly. We can let experience be our guide in the new world age where we will know directly for ourselves the mysteries of the soul and universe.

The modern science of enlightenment is in its early infancy as Spiritual psychology and further neurological studies are needed to observe the brain patterns of enlightened masters. In the age of knowing (gnosis) enlightenment will be the norm and not the exception to the rule as it was in man's previous golden ages.

If you are having doubts about enlightenment, this is a normal egotistical reaction to seeking God and the truth for yourself but remember enlightenment is a win-win situation as there are no losers (except for the ego & evil).

Enlightened people are often put on a pedestal as people have preconceived ideas about what an enlightened or spiritual person should be. These preconceived ideas are of the ego and we should not judge people based on their actions as they may be going through life lessons that are part of their path as there is much to learn after becoming enlightened and some of the lessons that life has to teach can be really challenging.

Life is difficult as it is without passing judgement on others. When we pass judgement on others with negative thoughts, feelings or words these forms of negative energy have a negative impact on the behaviour and actions of others as our thoughts, feelings, words and actions have the power to create or destroy life.

"Words kill, words give life; they're either poison or fruit - you choose." - Proverbs 18:21 (MSG)

The mind is the medium in which the word and energy is conveyed and must be treated with the upmost due care and attention for the power that they have. The word whether written, spoken or thought of is the most powerful form of magic that exists and it was through the word that God created the universe.

"In the beginning was the Word, and the Word was with God, and the Word was God." - John 1:1 (NIV)

It will be interesting to see how much of a better world we will live in after learning how to forgive ourselves and others and live a compassionate life free from sin and suffering and in line with our true nature.

Enlightenment is the only way to bring peace on earth and it will create a world free from sin and suffering and give us the luxury of exploring God, ourselves and the universe deeper than ever before.

With love

Chris T

THE WAY OF EMOTION

Author's foreword

Initiates, T. (1908). *The Kybalion: A Study of the Hermetic Philosophy of Ancient Egypt and Greece*. Chicago, Illinois: The Yogi Publication Society.

Frawley, D. (2006). *Yoga and the Sacred Fire: Self-Realization and Planetary Transformation*. Motilal Banarsidass Publishers.

Greer, M. K. (2002). *The Complete Book of Tarot Reversals*. Llewellyn Worldwide.

Introduction

What is Emotion?

Carey, G. W., & Perry, I. E. (1989). *The Zodiac and the Salts of Salvation: Homeopathic Remedies for the Sign Types*. Red Wheel/Weiser.

Russell, W. (1974). *The Universal One*. Swannanoa, Waynesboro, Virginia: University of Science and Philosophy.

Charry, J. M. (2018). *Air Ions: Physical and Biological Aspects*. Boca Raton, FL: CRC Press.

Macomber, S. (2013). *OUR ELECTRIC EMOTIONS*. Author Solutions.

Fisher, H. (2005). *Why we love: The nature and chemistry of romantic love*. New York: H. Holt.

Keown, D. (2013). *Buddhism: A Very Short Introduction*. Oxford: Oxford University Press.

Harvey, P. (2013). *An Introduction to Buddhism: Teachings, History and Practices*. Cambridge: Cambridge University Press.

Russell, W. (1947). *The Secret of Light*. Swannanoa, Waynesboro, Virginia: University of Science and Philosophy.

Wang, R. R. (2012). *Yinyang: The Way of Heaven and Earth in Chinese Thought and Culture*. Cambridge: Cambridge University Press.

Schulkin, J., & Schulkin, R. P. P. B. J. (2004). *Allostasis, Homeostasis, and the Costs of Physiological Adaptation*. Cambridge: Cambridge University Press.

Lazarus, R.S., & Folkman, S. (1984). *Stress, Appraisal and Coping*. New York: Springer Publishing Company.

Cannon, W.B. (1932). *The Wisdom of the Body*. W.W. New York: Norton.

Selye, H. (1985). History and present status of the stress concept. *In* A. Monat & R.S. Lazarus, eds. *Stress and Coping*, 2nd ed. New York: Columbia University.

Georgiadis, J. R., & Kringelbach, M. L. (2012). The human sexual response cycle: brain imaging evidence linking sex to other pleasures. *Progress in Neurobiology*, 98 (1), 49–81.

Langley, L. (2011). *Crazy little thing: How love and sex drive us mad*. Berkeley, Calif: Viva Editions.

"And if a kingdom be divided against itself, that kingdom cannot stand."
(Mark 3:24, King James Version).

G, Instructor. (2008, December 17). The Garden of Eden (2). *Kabbalah of Genesis, a Free Online Course*. Retrieved from https://gnosticteachings.org/courses/kabbalah-of-genesis/704-the-garden-of-eden-2.html

Tung, W.-C., & Li, Z. (2015). Pain Beliefs and Behaviors Among Chinese. *Home Health Care Management & Practice*, 27 (2), 95–97.

Wilson, E. (2012). *Emotions and Spirituality in Religions and Spiritual Movements*. Lanham, Md: University Press of America.

"When the even was come, they brought unto him many that were possessed with devils: and he cast out the spirits with his word, and healed all that were sick:"
(Matthew 6:18, King James Version).

Wycliffe, J., Swinburn, L. M., & British Library. (1917). *The Lanterne of light*. London: Published for the Early English Text Society by K. Paul, Trench, Trubner and Oxford University Press.

Tashi, T., Thubten, Z., & McDougall, G. (2006). *Buddhist psychology*. Boston: Wisdom Publications.

Graham, B. K. (2011). *Think, Believe, Receive: Three Steps to an Amazing Life*. Bloomington, IN: Balboa Press.

Stinson, A. (2008). *The Universe Of Reality: A Guidebook to Principle*. iUniverse.

Chapter 2

Rest

Goldstein, D. S., & Kopin, I. J. (2007). Evolution of concepts of stress. *Stress*, 10 (2), 109–120.

Schulkin, J., & Schulkin, R. P. P. B. J. (2004). *Allostasis, Homeostasis, and the Costs of Physiological Adaptation*. Cambridge: Cambridge University Press.

Lazarus, R.S., & Folkman, S. (1984). *Stress, Appraisal and Coping*. New York: Springer Publishing Company.

Cannon, W.B. (1932). *The Wisdom of the Body*. W.W. New York: Norton.

Selye, H. (1985). History and present status of the stress concept. *In* A. Monat & R.S. Lazarus, eds. *Stress and Coping*, 2nd ed. New York: Columbia University.

Starr, C., & McMillan, B. (2006). *Human Biology*. Cengage Learning.

Stress

Russell, W. (1947). *The Secret of Light*. Swannanoa, Waynesboro, Virginia: University of Science and Philosophy.

Shumsky, S. (2015). *Awaken Your Third Eye: How Accessing Your Sixth Sense Can Help You Find Knowledge, Illumination, and Intuition*. Red Wheel/Weiser.

Bernard, L. C., & Krupat, E. (1994). *Health Psychology: Biopsychosocial Factors in Health and Illness*. New York: Harcourt Brace College Publishers.

Cannon, W.B. (1932). *The Wisdom of the Body*. W.W. New York: Norton.

Selye, H. (1985). History and present status of the stress concept. *In* A. Monat & R.S. Lazarus, eds. *Stress and Coping*, 2nd ed. New York: Columbia University.

Selye, H. (1956). *The Stress of Life*. New York: McGraw-Hill.

Selye, H. (1976). *Stress in health and disease*. Reading, MA: Butterworth.

Selye, H. (1982). History and present status of the stress concept. *In* L. Goldberger and S. Breznitz (Eds). *Handbook of stress: Theoretical and clinical aspects*. New York: The Free Press.

Selye, H. (1975). Confusion and controversy in the stress field. *Journal of Human Stress*, 1 (2), 37–44.

Gandee, R. N., Knierim, H., & McLittle-Marino, D. (1998). Stress and older adults: a mind-body relationship. Journal of Physical Education, Recreation & Dance, 69 (9), 19-22.

Lazarus, R.S., & Folkman, S. (1984). *Stress, Appraisal and Coping*. New York: Springer Publishing Company.

Lazarus, R.S., & Launier, R. (1978). Stress-related transactions between person and environment. *In* L. A. Pervin & M. Lewis, eds. *Perspectives in Interactional Psychology*. New York: Plenum.

Dienstbier, R.A., (1989). Arousal and physiological toughness: Implications for mental and physical health. *Psychological Review,* 96 (1), 84–100.

Frankenhaeuser M. (1986) A Psychobiological Framework for Research on Human Stress and Coping. In: Appley M.H., Trumbull R. (eds) *Dynamics of Stress. The Plenum Series on Stress and Coping*. Boston, MA: Springer.

Edwards, D. C. (1999). *Motivation and Emotion*. Thousand Oaks, Calif: SAGE Publications.

Cannon, W.B. (1915). *Bodily changes in pain, hunger, fear, and rage*. New York: Appleton-Century-Crofts.

Pfaff, D. (2009). *Brain Arousal and Information Theory: Neural and Genetic Mechanisms*. Cambridge: Harvard University Press.

Lewis, K. D. S., & Bear, B. J. (2009). *Manual of school health: A handbook for school nurses, educators, and health professionals.* Philadelphia, Pa: Saunders.

Mischoulon, D., & Rosenbaum, J. F. (2002). *Natural medications and the treatment of psychiatric disorders: Considering the alternatives.* Philadelphia: Lippincott Williams & Wilkins.

Berridge C. W. (2007). Noradrenergic modulation of arousal. *Brain research reviews,* 58 (1), 1-17.

Noudoost, B., & Moore, T. (2011). The role of neuromodulators in selective attention. *Trends in cognitive sciences, 15* (12), 585-91.

Thayer, R. E. (1997). *The Origin of Everyday Moods: Managing Energy, Tension, and Stress.* Oxford: Oxford University Press.

Thakkar M. M. (2011). Histamine in the regulation of wakefulness. *Sleep medicine reviews, 15* (1), 65-74.

Jansen, A. S., Van Nguyen, X., Karpitskiy, V., Mettenleiter, T. C., & Loewy, A. D. (1995). Central command neurons of the sympathetic nervous system: basis of the fight-or-flight response. *Science, 270* (5236), 644-646.

Rea, P. (2016). *Essential clinically applied anatomy of the peripheral nervous system in the head and neck.* Academic Press.

Willis, W. D. (2007). GABA Mechanisms and Descending Inhibitory Mechanisms. *Encyclopedia of Pain,* 814-817.

Watson, C. J., Baghdoyan, H. A., & Lydic, R. (2010). Neuropharmacology of sleep and wakefulness. *Sleep medicine clinics, 5* (4), 513-528.

Samardzic, J., Jadzic, D., Hencic, B., Jancic, J., & Strac, D. S. (2018). Introductory Chapter: GABA/Glutamate Balance: A Key for Normal Brain Functioning. GABA And Glutamate: *New Developments In Neurotransmission Research,* 1.

Lydiard, R. B. (2003). The role of GABA in anxiety disorders. *The Journal of clinical psychiatry, 64,* 21-27.

Abdou, A. M., Higashiguchi, S., Horie, K., Kim, M., Hatta, H., & Yokogoshi, H. (2006). Relaxation and immunity enhancement effects of γ-Aminobutyric acid (GABA) administration in humans. *Biofactors, 26* (3), 201-208.

Chapter 3

Excitement

McMillan, D. W. (2013). *Emotion Rituals: A resource for therapists and clients.* New York: Routledge.

Karoly, P. P. P., Karoly, P., & Kanfer, F. H. (1982). *Self-management and Behavior Change: From Theory to Practice.* Pergamon Press.

Coon, D., & Mitterer, J. O. (2013). *Psychology: A Journey*. Belmont, Calif: Wadsworth/Cengage Learning.

Omary, M. A., & Patterson, H. H. (1999). Luminescence, Theory*. In J. C. Lindon (Ed.), *Encyclopedia of Spectroscopy and Spectrometry (Second Edition)* (Second Edition, pp. 1372–1391). Academic Press.

Selye, Hans (1974). *Stress without distress*. Philadelphia: J.B. Lippincott Company.

Selye, H. (1975). Confusion and controversy in the stress field. *Journal of Human Stress*, 1 (2), 37–44.

Selye, H. (1975). Stress and distress. *Comprehensive therapy*, *1* (8), 9-13.

Wolfe, D. (2012). *Naked Chocolate: The Astonishing Truth About the World's Greatest Food*. North Atlantic Books.

Sabelli, H. C., & Javaid, J. I. (1995). Phenylethylamine modulation of affect: therapeutic and diagnostic implications. *The Journal of Neuropsychiatry and Clinical Neurosciences*, *7* (1), 6–14.

Sabelli, H., Fink, P., Fawcett, J., & Tom, C. (1996). Sustained antidepressant effect of PEA replacement. *The Journal of Neuropsychiatry and Clinical Neurosciences*, 8 (2), 168–171.

Thayer, R. E. (1997). *The origin of everyday moods: Managing energy, tension, and stress*. New York: Oxford University Press.

Kahn, R. S., van Praag, H. M., Wetzler, S., Asnis, G. M., & Barr, G. (1988). Serotonin and anxiety revisited. *Biological Psychiatry*, *23* (2), 189–208.

Harmer, C. J., Duman, R. S., & Cowen, P. J. (2017). How do antidepressants work? New perspectives for refining future treatment approaches. *The lancet. Psychiatry*, *4* (5), 409-418.

Childs, G. (1995). *Understand your temperament*. London: Sophia.

Eysenck, H. J. (1967). *The biological basis of personality*. Springfield, Ill: C.C. Thomas.

Ekstrand, D. W. (2018, September 25). *THE FOUR HUMAN TEMPERAMENTS*. Retrieved from http://www.thetransformedsoul.com/additional-studies/miscellaneous-studies/the-four-human-temperaments.

Neurochemistry & Physiology

Martin, E. M., & Pfaff, D. W. (2013). Elementary CNS Arousal. *Neuroscience in the 21st Century: From Basic to Clinical*, 2147-2171.

Edlow, B. L., Takahashi, E., Wu, O., Benner, T., Dai, G., Bu, L., ... & Folkerth, R. D. (2012). Neuroanatomic connectivity of the human ascending arousal system critical to consciousness and its disorders. *Journal of Neuropathology & Experimental Neurology*, *71* (6), 531-546.

McMillan, D. W. (2013). *Emotion Rituals: A resource for therapists and clients*. New York: Routledge.

Micheli, L. J. (2011). *Encyclopedia of sports medicine*. Thousand Oaks, Calif: SAGE Publications.

Hart, A., & Recorded Books, Inc. (1995). *Adrenaline And Stress: The Exciting New Breakthrough That Helps You Overcome Stress Damage*. Nashville, Tennessee: Thomas Nelson.

Fisher, H. E. (1992). *Anatomy of love: A natural history of mating, marriage, and why we stray*. New York: Fawcett Columbine.

Bamba, P. A. (2010). *Perfect marriage, not a mirage: A journey through ups and downs of marriage*. New Delhi: Pustak Mahal.

Wolfe, D. (2012). *Naked Chocolate: The Astonishing Truth About the World's Greatest Food*. North Atlantic Books.

Sabelli, H. C., & Javaid, J. I. (1995). Phenylethylamine modulation of affect: therapeutic and diagnostic implications. *The Journal of Neuropsychiatry and Clinical Neurosciences*, *7* (1), 6–14.

Sabelli, H., Fink, P., Fawcett, J., & Tom, C. (1996). Sustained antidepressant effect of PEA replacement. *The Journal of Neuropsychiatry and Clinical Neurosciences*, 8 (2), 168–171.

Valter, K., Arrizabalaga, P., & Landry, J. C. (1998). *Designer Drugs Directory*. Elsevier Science.

Kovacic, P., & Somanathan, R. (2009). Novel, unifying mechanism for mescaline in the central nervous system: electrochemistry, catechol redox metabolite, receptor, cell signaling and structure activity relationships. *Oxidative medicine and cellular longevity*, *2* (4), 181-90.

Hurst, W. J., & Toomey, P. B. (1981). High-performance liquid chromatographic determination of four biogenic amines in chocolate. *Analyst*, *106* (1261), 394-402.

Hodgson, E., & Roe, M. (2014). *Dictionary of Toxicology*. Elsevier Science.

McCulloch, J., & Harper, A. M. (1977). Phenylethylamine and cerebral blood flow. Possible involvement of phenylethylamine in migraine. *Neurology*, *27* (9), 817–821.

Szabo, A., Billett, E., & Turner, J. (2001). Phenylethylamine, a possible link to the antidepressant effects of exercise? *British Journal of Sports Medicine*, *35* (5), 342-343.

Janssen, P. A. J., Leysen, J. E., Megens, A. A. H. P., & Awouters, F. H. L. (1999). Does phenylethylamine act as an endogenous amphetamine in some patients? *The International Journal of Neuropsychopharmacology*, *2* (3), 229–240.

Sandler, M., & Reynolds, G. (1976). Does phenylethylamine cause schizophrenia? *Lancet*, *1*, 70–71.

Baker, G. B., Bornstein, R. A., Rouget, A. C., Ashton, S. E., van Muyden, J. C., & Coutts, R. (1991). Phenylethylaminergic mechanisms in attention-deficit disorder. *Biological Psychiatry, 29*, 15–22.

Kusaga, A. (2002). Decreased β-phenylethylamine in urine of children with attention deficit hyperactivity disorder and autistic disorder. *No to Hattatsu. Brain and Development, 34*, 243–248.

Kusaga, A., Yamashita, Y., Koeda, T., Hiratani, M., Kaneko, M., Yamada, S., & Matsuishi, T. (2002). Increased urine phenylethylamine after methylphenidate treatment in children with ADHD. *Annals of Neurology, 52*, 372–374.

Potter, P. M. (2007). Growing Beyond Our Genetics: Adolescence and Beyond. Lulu.com.

Smith, A., Brice, C., Nash, J., Rich, N., & Nutt, D. J. (2003). Caffeine and central noradrenaline: effects on mood, cognitive performance, eye movements and cardiovascular function. *Journal of psychopharmacology, 17* (3), 283-292.

Thayer, R. E. (1997). *The origin of everyday moods: Managing energy, tension, and stress.* New York: Oxford University Press.

Kahn, R. S., van Praag, H. M., Wetzler, S., Asnis, G. M., & Barr, G. (1988). Serotonin and anxiety revisited. *Biological Psychiatry, 23* (2), 189–208.

Harmer, C. J., Duman, R. S., & Cowen, P. J. (2017). How do antidepressants work? New perspectives for refining future treatment approaches. *The lancet. Psychiatry, 4* (5), 409-418.

Vingerhoets, A. (2013). *Why Only Humans Weep: Unravelling the Mysteries of Tears.* Oxford: Oxford University Press.

Roth, B. L. (1994). Multiple serotonin receptors: clinical and experimental aspects. *Annals of Clinical Psychiatry: Official Journal of the American Academy of Clinical Psychiatrists, 6* (2), 67–78.

Robinson, O. J., Cools, R., Crockett, M. J., & Sahakian, B. J. (2010). Mood state moderates the role of serotonin in cognitive biases. *Journal of Psychopharmacology (Oxford, England), 24* (4), 573–583.

Gray, J. R., Braver, T. S., & Raichle, M. E. (2002). Integration of emotion and cognition in the lateral prefrontal cortex. *Proceedings of the National Academy of Sciences, 99* (6), 4115-4120.

Ramasubbu, R. (2001). Dose-response relationship of selective serotonin reuptake inhibitors treatment-emergent hypomania in depressive disorders. *Acta Psychiatrica Scandinavica, 104* (3), 236–239.

Dolan, B., & Holt, L. (2008). *Accident and emergency: Theory into practice.* Edinburgh: Bailliere Tindall Elsevier.

Perception & Modality

Russell, W. (1974). *The Universal One.* Swannanoa, Waynesboro, Virginia: University of Science and Philosophy.

Leeming, D. A., & Leeming, D. A. (2010). *Creation myths of the world: An encyclopedia.* Santa Barbara, Calif: ABC-CLIO.

Langley, L. (2011). *Crazy little thing: How love and sex drive us mad.* Berkeley, Calif: Viva Editions.

Newell, R., & Gournay, K. (2008). *Mental Health Nursing: An Evidence Based Approach.* London: Elsevier Health Sciences UK.

Tariri, B. (2013). *Desexed.* Author House.

Volkow, N. D., Fowler, J. S., Wang, G. J., Baler, R., & Telang, F. (2008). Imaging dopamine's role in drug abuse and addiction. *Neuropharmacology, 56 Suppl 1* (Suppl 1), 3–8.

Georgiadis, J. R., & Kringelbach, M. L. (2012). The human sexual response cycle: brain imaging evidence linking sex to other pleasures. *Progress in Neurobiology,* 98 (1), 49–81.

Siegel, S., & Allan, L. G. (1998). Learning and homeostasis: drug addiction and the McCollough effect. *Psychological Bulletin,* 124 (2), 230–239.

Taylor, J., & Wilson, G. S. (2005). *Applying sport psychology: Four perspectives.* Champaign, IL: Human.

Goleman, D. (1995). *Emotional Intelligence.* London: Bantam Books.

Chapter 4

Fear

Fear. (n.d.). *Farlex Partner Medical Dictionary.* Retrieved January 22, 2020, from https://medical-dictionary.thefreedictionary.com/fear.

Selye, H. (1984). *The Stress of Life.* New York: McGraw-Hill.

Selye, H. (1985). History and present status of the stress concept. *In* A. Monat & R.S. Lazarus, eds. *Stress and Coping,* 2nd ed. New York: Columbia University.

Selye, H. (1976). *Stress in health and disease.* Reading, MA: Butterworth.

Selye, H. (1982). History and present status of the stress concept. *In* L. Goldberger and S. Breznitz (Eds). *Handbook of stress: Theoretical and clinical aspects.* New York: The Free Press.

Selye, H. (1975). Confusion and controversy in the stress field. *Journal of Human Stress,* 1 (2), 37–44.

Cannon, W.B. (1915). *Bodily changes in pain, hunger, fear, and rage.* New York: Appleton-Century-Crofts.

Cannon, W.B. (1932). *The Wisdom of the Body*. W.W. New York: Norton.

Olsson, A., & Phelps, E. A. (2007). Social learning of fear. *Nature Neuroscience*, 10 (9), 1095–1102.

Lazarus, R.S., & Folkman, S. (1984). *Stress, Appraisal and Coping*. New York: Springer.

Lazarus, R.S., & Launier, R. (1978). Stress-related transactions between person and environment. *In* L. A. Pervin & M. Lewis, eds. *Perspectives in Interactional Psychology*. New York: Plenum.

Lewis, M., Haviland-Jones, J. M., & Barrett, L. F. (2010). *Handbook of emotions*. New York: Guilford Press.

Phelps, E. A., & LeDoux, J. E. (2005). Contributions of the amygdala to emotion processing: from animal models to human behavior. *Neuron, 48* (2), 175–187.

Tran, L., Lasher, B. K., Young, K. A., & Keele, N. B. (2013). Depletion of serotonin in the basolateral amygdala elevates glutamate receptors and facilitates fear-potentiated startle. *Translational Psychiatry, 3*, e298.

Stein, D. J., Hollander, E., & Rothbaum, B. O. (2009). *Textbook of Anxiety Disorders*. Washington, DC: American Psychiatric Publishing.

Davidson, R. J. (2003). Affective neuroscience and psychophysiology: Toward a synthesis. *Psychophysiology, 40* (5), 655–665.

Faith, R. E., Good, R. A., Murgo, A. J., & Plotnikoff, N. P. (2013). *Enkephalins and Endorphins: Stress and the Immune System*. New York: Springer.

Dfarhud, D., Malmir, M., & Khanahmadi, M. (2014). Happiness & Health: The Biological Factors- Systematic Review Article. *Iranian journal of public health, 43* (11), 1468–1477.

Neurochemistry & Physiology

Goleman, D. (1995). *Emotional Intelligence*. London: Bantam Books.

Van Diest, I., Bradley, M. M., Guerra, P., Van den Bergh, O., & Lang, P. J. (2008). Fear-conditioned respiration and its association to cardiac reactivity. *Biological psychology, 80* (2), 212–217.

Bloodstone, J. D. (2013). *Think & Grow Balls!: How to Shrink Your Fear & Enlarge Your Courage*. Lulu.com.

Bayless, S. J., Glover, M., Taylor, M. J., & Itier, R. J. (2011). Is it in the eyes? Dissociating the role of emotion and perceptual features of emotionally expressive faces in modulating orienting to eye gaze. *Visual cognition*, 19 (4), 483-510.

Edmundson, L. M. (2018, September 20). *The Neurobiology of Fear*. Retrieved from https://serendipstudio.org/bb/neuro/neuro00/web2/Edmundson.html

Bezdek, K. G., & Telzer, E. H. (2017). Have no fear, the brain is here! How your brain responds to stress. *Front. Young Minds, 5*, 71.

Herman, J. P., McKlveen, J. M., Ghosal, S., Kopp, B., Wulsin, A., Makinson, R., Myers, B. (2016). Regulation of the Hypothalamic-Pituitary-Adrenocortical Stress Response. *Comprehensive Physiology*, *6* (2), 603–621.

Swanson, L. W. (2000). Cerebral hemisphere regulation of motivated behavior. *Brain Research*, *886* (1–2), 113–164.

Cohen, N. J., & Eichenbaum, H. (1993). Memory, amnesia, and the hippocampal system. In *Memory, amnesia, and the hippocampal system*. Cambridge, MA, US: The MIT Press.

Squire, L. R., & Schacter, D. L. (Eds.). (2002). Neuropsychology of memory, 3rd ed. *Neuropsychology of Memory, 3rd Ed.*, pp. xviii, 519–xviii, 519. New York: The Guilford Press.

Rubin, R. D., Watson, P. D., Duff, M. C., & Cohen, N. J. (2014). The role of the hippocampus in flexible cognition and social behavior. *Frontiers in Human Neuroscience*, 8, 742.

Schiraldi, G. R. (2016). *The Post-Traumatic Stress Disorder Sourcebook, Revised and Expanded Second Edition: A Guide to Healing, Recovery, and Growth: A Guide to Healing, Recovery, and Growth*. New York, NY: McGraw-Hill Education.

Akirav, I., & Maroun, M. (2007). The role of the medial prefrontal cortex-amygdala circuit in stress effects on the extinction of fear. *Neural plasticity*, *2007*, 30873.

Samuelson K. W. (2011). Post-traumatic stress disorder and declarative memory functioning: a review. *Dialogues in clinical neuroscience*, 13 (3), 346–351.

Davidson, R. J. (2003). Affective neuroscience and psychophysiology: Toward a synthesis. *Psychophysiology*, *40* (5), 655–665.

Peluso, M. A. M., Glahn, D. C., Matsuo, K., Monkul, E. S., Najt, P., Zamarripa, F., Soares, J. C. (2009). Amygdala hyperactivation in untreated depressed individuals. *Psychiatry Research*, *173* (2), 158–161.

Tran, L., Lasher, B. K., Young, K. A., & Keele, N. B. (2013). Depletion of serotonin in the basolateral amygdala elevates glutamate receptors and facilitates fear-potentiated startle. *Translational Psychiatry*, *3*, e298.

Stein, D. J., Hollander, E., & Rothbaum, B. O. (2009). *Textbook of Anxiety Disorders*. Washington, DC: American Psychiatric Publishing.

Mezzacappa, E. S. (1999). Epinephrine, Arousal, and Emotion: A New Look at Two-factor Theory. *Cognition and Emotion*, *13* (2), 181–199.

Goldstein D. S. (2010). Adrenal responses to stress. *Cellular and molecular neurobiology*, *30* (8), 1433–1440.

Urry, H. L., Nitschke, J. B., Dolski, I., Jackson, D. C., Dalton, K. M., Mueller, C. J., Davidson, R. J. (2004). *Making a Life Worth Living: Neural Correlates of Well-Being. Psychological Science*, 15 (6), 367–372.

Davidson, J. R. T. (2000). Trauma: The Impact of Post-Traumatic Stress Disorder. *Journal of Psychopharmacology*, *14* (2_suppl1), S5–S12.

Lane, R. D., & Nadel, L. (2002). *Cognitive Neuroscience of Emotion*. Oxford: Oxford University Press.

Bracha, H. S., Garcia-Rill, E., Mrak, R. E., & Skinner, R. (2005). Postmortem locus coeruleus neuron count in three American veterans with probable or possible war-related PTSD. *The Journal of Neuropsychiatry and Clinical Neurosciences*, 17 (4), 503–509.

Perception & Modality

Selye, H. (1984). *The Stress of Life*. New York: McGraw-Hill.

Selye, H. (1985). History and present status of the stress concept. *In* A. Monat & R.S. Lazarus, eds. *Stress and Coping*, 2nd ed. New York: Columbia University.

Selye, H. (1976). *Stress in health and disease*. Reading, MA: Butterworth.

Selye, H. (1982). History and present status of the stress concept. *In* L. Goldberger and S. Breznitz (Eds). *Handbook of stress: Theoretical and clinical aspects*. New York: The Free Press.

Selye, H. (1975). Confusion and controversy in the stress field. *Journal of Human Stress*, 1 (2), 37–44.

Cannon, W.B. (1915). *Bodily changes in pain, hunger, fear, and rage*. New York: Appleton-Century-Crofts.

Cannon, W.B. (1932). *The Wisdom of the Body*. W.W. New York: Norton.

Lazarus, R.S., & Folkman, S. (1984). *Stress, Appraisal and Coping*. New York: Springer Publishing Company.

Lazarus, R.S., & Launier, R. (1978). Stress-related transactions between person and environment. *In* L. A. Pervin & M. Lewis, eds. *Perspectives in Interactional Psychology*. New York: Plenum.

McMillan, D. W. (2013). *Emotion Rituals: A resource for therapists and clients*. New York: Routledge.

Goleman, D. (1995). *Emotional Intelligence*. London: Bantam Books.

Batmaz, S., Ahmet Yuncu, O., & Kocbiyik, S. (2015). Assessing Negative Automatic Thoughts: Psychometric Properties of the Turkish Version of the Cognition Checklist. *Iranian Journal of Psychiatry and Behavioral Sciences*, 9 (4), e3444.

Tucker, Michele. (2015). *False Evidence Appearing Real*. Authorhouse.

Chapter 5

Anger

Videbeck, S. L. (2006). *Psychiatric Mental Health Nursing*. Philadelphia: Lippincott Williams & Wilkins.

DiGiuseppe, R., & Tafrate, R. C. (2006). *Understanding Anger Disorders*. Oxford: Oxford University Press.

Fink, G. (2000). *Encyclopedia of Stress*. London: Academic Press.

Nevid, J. S. (2011). *Essentials of Psychology: Concepts and Applications*. Belmont, Calif: Cengage Learning.

Cannon, W.B. (1932). *The Wisdom of the Body*. W.W. New York: Norton.

Selye, H. (1985). History and present status of the stress concept. *In* A. Monat & R.S. Lazarus, eds. *Stress and Coping*, 2nd ed. New York: Columbia University.

Selye, H. (1956). *The Stress of Life*. New York: McGraw-Hill.

Selye, H. (1976). *Stress in health and disease.* Reading, MA: Butterworth.

Selye, H. (1982). History and present status of the stress concept. *In* L. Goldberger and S. Breznitz (Eds). *Handbook of stress: Theoretical and clinical aspects.* New York: The Free Press.

Selye, H. (1975). Confusion and controversy in the stress field. *Journal of Human Stress*, 1 (2), 37–44.

McMillan, D. W. (2013). *Emotion Rituals: A resource for therapists and clients.* New York: Routledge.

Fischer, A. G., & Ullsperger, M. (2017). An Update on the Role of Serotonin and its Interplay with Dopamine for Reward. *Frontiers in human neuroscience*, 11, 484.

Burns, D. J. (2018). *Multifaceted Explorations of Consumer Culture and Its Impact on Individuals and Society*. IGI Global.

Ekstrand, D. W. (2018, September 25). *THE FOUR HUMAN TEMPERAMENTS*. Retrieved from http://www.thetransformedsoul.com/additional-studies/miscellaneous-studies/the-four-human-temperaments.

Childs, G. (1995). *Understand your temperament*. London: Sophia.

Eysenck, H. J. (1967). *The biological basis of personality*. Springfield, Ill: C.C. Thomas.

Neurochemistry & Physiology

Fink, G. (2000). *Encyclopedia of Stress*. London: Academic Press.

Bhave, S. Y., & Saini, S. (2009). *Anger Management*. India: SAGE Publications.

McMillan, D. W. (2013). *Emotion Rituals: A resource for therapists and clients*. New York: Routledge.

Pivonello, R., Ferone, D., De Herder, W. W., De Krijger, R. R., Waaijers, M., Mooij, D. M., & Colao, A. (2004). Dopamine receptor expression and function in human normal adrenal gland and adrenal tumors. *The Journal of Clinical Endocrinology & Metabolism*,

89 (9), 4493-4502.

Duggirala, R., Almasy, L., Williams-Blangero, S., Paul, S. F. D., & Kole, C. (2015). *Genome Mapping and Genomics in Human and Non-Human Primates*. Berlin, Heidelberg: Springer Berlin Heidelberg.

Fink, G. (2010). *Stress Consequences: Mental, Neuropsychological and Socioeconomic*. London: Academic Press.

Batrinos, M. L. (2012). Testosterone and Aggressive Behavior in Man. *International Journal of Endocrinology and Metabolism, 10* (3), 563–568.

DiGiuseppe, R., & Tafrate, R. C. (2006). *Understanding Anger Disorders*. Oxford: Oxford University Press.

Mischoulon, D., & Rosenbaum, J. F. (2002). *Natural medications and the treatment of psychiatric disorders: Considering the alternatives*. Philadelphia: Lippincott Williams & Wilkins.

Broderick, E. D., & Crosby, B. (2018). Anticholinergic Toxicity. In *StatPearls [Internet]*. StatPearls Publishing.

Banks, S. J., Eddy, K. T., Angstadt, M., Nathan, P. J., & Phan, K. L. (2007). Amygdala-frontal connectivity during emotion regulation. *Social cognitive and affective neuroscience*, 2 (4), 303–312.

Moran, M. (2016). *All the Rage: A Quest*. Beacon Press.

Wallis, G. (2007). *Basic Teachings of the Buddha*. Random House Publishing Group.

Sunderland, M., & Hancock, N. (2017). *Draw on Your Relationships: Creative Ways to Explore, Understand and Work Through Important Relationship Issues*. Routledge.

Catalano, J. T. (2015). *Nursing now! Today's issues, tomorrow's trends*. Philadelphia, PA: F. A. Davis Company.

Leggett, A. N., Zarit, S. H., Kim, K., Almeida, D. M., & Klein, L. C. (2014). Depressive Mood, Anger, and Daily Cortisol of Caregivers on High- and Low-Stress Days. *The journals of gerontology. Series B, Psychological sciences and social sciences, 70* (6), 820–829.

Sharon L. Lewis, R. N. P. D. F., Bucher, L., Margaret M. Heitkemper, R. N. P. D. F., & Dirksen, S. R. (2013). *Medical-Surgical Nursing: Assessment and Management of Clinical Problems, Single Volume*. St. Louis, Missouri: Elsevier/Mosby.

Mischoulon, D., & Rosenbaum, J. F. (2008). *Natural Medications for Psychiatric Disorders: Considering the Alternatives*. Philadelphia: Lippincott Williams & Wilkins.

Chaouloff, F., Berton, O., & Mormède, P. (1999). Serotonin and stress. *Neuropsychopharmacology, 21* (1), 28-32.

Hoffman, L., Watson, P. B., Wilson, G., & Montgomery, J. (1989). Low plasma β-endorphin in post-traumatic stress disorder. *Australian & New Zealand Journal of Psychiatry, 23* (2), 269-273.

Adams, J. G. (2012). *Emergency Medicine E-Book: Clinical Essentials (Expert Consult -- Online)*. Philadelphia, PA: Elsevier Health Sciences.

Suzuki, Y., Itoh, H., Amada, K., Yamamura, R., Sato, Y., & Takeyama, M. (2013). Significant Increase in Salivary Substance P Level after a Single Oral Dose of Cevimeline in Humans. *International Journal of Peptides*, *2013*, 284765.

Botvinick, M., Nystrom, L. E., Fissell, K., Carter, C. S., & Cohen, J. D. (1999). Conflict monitoring versus selection-for-action in anterior cingulate cortex. *Nature*, *402* (6758), 179–181.

Bush, G., Luu, P., & Posner, M. I. (2000). Cognitive and emotional influences in anterior cingulate cortex. *Trends in cognitive sciences*, *4* (6), 215-222.

Pardo, J. V., Pardo, P. J., Janer, K. W., & Raichle, M. E. (1990). The anterior cingulate cortex mediates processing selection in the Stroop attentional conflict paradigm. *Proceedings of the National Academy of Sciences*, *87* (1), 256-259.

Eisenberger, N. I., Lieberman, M. D., & Williams, K. D. (2003). Does rejection hurt? An fMRI study of social exclusion. *Science*, *302* (5643), 290-292.

Klimecki, O. M., Sander, D., & Vuilleumier, P. (2018). Distinct brain areas involved in anger versus punishment during social interactions. *Scientific reports*, *8* (1), 10556.

Boulton, A. A., Baker, G. B., Dewhurst, W. G., & Sandler, M. (2013). *Neurobiology of the Trace Amines: Analytical, Physiological, Pharmacological, Behavioral, and Clinical Aspects*. Clifton, N.J: Humana Press.

Perception & Modality

Kassinove, H. (2014). *Anger Disorders: Definition, Diagnosis, And Treatment*. Hoboken: Taylor & Francis.

Kazdin, A. E. (2000). *Encyclopedia of Psychology: Table-zubin*. Washington, D.C: American Psychological Association.

In, I. (2016). *The International Journal of Indian Psychology, Volume 3, Issue 4, No. 65*. Lulu & RED'SHINE Publication. Inc.

McMillan, D. W. (2013). *Emotion Rituals: A resource for therapists and clients*. New York: Routledge.

Sturgeon, J. A., & Zautra, A. J. (2015). Social pain and physical pain: shared paths to resilience. *Pain management*, *6* (1), 63–74.

Santrock, J. (2011). *A Topical Approach to Life-Span Development*. McGraw-Hill. Education.

Bowlby, J. (1973). *Attachment and Loss: Separation: anxiety and anger*. New York: Basic Books.

Elisabeth Kubler-Ross, D. K. (2014). *On Grief and Grieving: Finding the Meaning of Grief Through the Five Stages of Loss*. New York: Simon & Schuster UK.

Boulton, A. A., Baker, G. B., Dewhurst, W. G., & Sandler, M. (2013). *Neurobiology of the Trace Amines: Analytical, Physiological, Pharmacological, Behavioral, and Clinical Aspects.* Clifton, N.J: Humana Press.

Chapter 6

Desire

McMillan, D. W. (2013). *Emotion Rituals: A resource for therapists and clients.* New York: Routledge.

Martinich, A. P., & Hobbes, T. (1998). *A Hobbes dictionary.* Malden, Mass: Blackwell.

Kawabata H, Zeki S (2008) The Neural Correlates of Desire. *PLOS ONE 3 (8)*: e3027.

Cannon, W.B. (1932). *The Wisdom of the Body.* W.W. New York: Norton.

Selye, H. (1985). History and present status of the stress concept. *In* A. Monat & R.S. Lazarus, eds. *Stress and Coping,* 2nd ed. New York: Columbia University.

Selye, H. (1956). *The Stress of Life.* New York: McGraw-Hill.

Selye, H. (1976). *Stress in health and disease.* Reading, MA: Butterworth.

Selye, H. (1982). History and present status of the stress concept. *In* L. Goldberger and S. Breznitz (Eds). *Handbook of stress: Theoretical and clinical aspects.* New York: The Free Press.

Selye, H. (1975). Confusion and controversy in the stress field. *Journal of Human Stress,* 1 (2), 37–44.

Lazarus, R.S., & Folkman, S. (1984). *Stress, Appraisal and Coping.* New York: Springer Publishing Company.

Selye, Hans (1974). *Stress without distress.* Philadelphia: J.B. Lippincott Company.

Lewis, T., Amini, F., & Lannon, R. (2000). *A General Theory of Love.* Random House.

Fischer, A. G., & Ullsperger, M. (2017). An Update on the Role of Serotonin and its Interplay with Dopamine for Reward. *Frontiers in human neuroscience,* 11, 484.

Puglisi-Allegra, S., & Andolina, D. (2015). Serotonin and stress coping. *Behavioural Brain Research, 277,* 58–67.

Neurochemistry & Physiology

Selye, H. (1975). Confusion and controversy in the stress field. *Journal of Human Stress,* 1 (2), 37–44.

Gandee, R. N., Knierim, H., & McLittle-Marino, D. (1998). Stress and older adults: a mind-body relationship. *Journal of Physical Education, Recreation & Dance, 69 (9),* 19-22.

Theorell, T. (2001). Occupational Health. In N. J. Smelser & P. B. Baltes (Eds.), *International Encyclopedia of the Social & Behavioral Sciences* (pp. 10828–10835).

Garrett, W. E., & Kirkendall, D. T. (2000). *Exercise and Sport Science*. Philadelphia: Lippincott Williams & Wilkins.

Ulrich-Lai, Y. M., & Herman, J. P. (2009). Neural regulation of endocrine and autonomic stress responses. *Nature reviews. Neuroscience, 10* (6), 397-409.

Fink, G. (2010). *Stress Consequences: Mental, Neuropsychological and Socioeconomic.* London: Academic Press.

Rodriguez-Martin, B. C., & Meule, A. (2015). *Food cravings*. S.L: Frontiers Media SA.

Coon, D. (1998). *Introduction to psychology: Exploration and application*. Pacific Grove, Calif: Brooks/Cole Pub.

Frankenhaeuser M. (1986) A Psychobiological Framework for Research on Human Stress and Coping. In: Appley M.H., Trumbull R. (eds) *Dynamics of Stress. The Plenum Series on Stress and Coping*. Boston, MA: Springer.

Lewis, K. D. S., & Bear, B. J. (2009). *Manual of school health: A handbook for school nurses, educators, and health professionals.* Philadelphia, Pa: Saunders.

Mischoulon, D., & Rosenbaum, J. F. (2002). *Natural medications and the treatment of psychiatric disorders: Considering the alternatives*. Philadelphia: Lippincott Williams & Wilkins.

Berridge C. W. (2007). Noradrenergic modulation of arousal. *Brain research reviews,* 58 (1), 1-17.

Noudoost, B., & Moore, T. (2011). The role of neuromodulators in selective attention. *Trends in cognitive sciences, 15* (12), 585-91.

Edwards, D. C. (1999). *Motivation and Emotion*. Thousand Oaks, Calif: SAGE Publications.

McMillan, D. W. (2013). *Emotion Rituals: A resource for therapists and clients*. New York: Routledge.

Fink, G. (2000). *Encyclopedia of Stress*. London: Academic Press.

Rieger, G., & Savin-Williams, R. C. (2012). The eyes have it: sex and sexual orientation differences in pupil dilation patterns. *PloS one, 7* (8), e40256.

Salamone, J. D., & Correa, M. (2012). The Mysterious Motivational Functions of Mesolimbic Dopamine. *Neuron, 76* (3), 470–485.

Curzon, G. (1990). Serotonin and appetite. *Annals of the New York Academy of Sciences*, 600, 521.

Stroebe, W., Papies, E. K., & Aarts, H. (2008). From Homeostatic to Hedonic Theories of Eating: Self-Regulatory Failure in Food-Rich Environments. *Applied Psychology*, 57 (s1), 172–193.

Pelchat, M. L., Johnson, A., Chan, R., Valdez, J., & Ragland, J. D. (2004). Images of desire: food-craving activation during fMRI. *NeuroImage, 23* (4), 1486–1493.

Kawabata, H., & Zeki, S. (2008). The Neural Correlates of Desire. *PLOS ONE, 3* (8), 1–9.

Bargmann, C. I., & Horvitz, H. R. (1991). Chemosensory neurons with overlapping functions direct chemotaxis to multiple chemicals in C. elegans. *Neuron, 7* (5), 729–742.

Bartels, A., & Zeki, S. (2000). The neural basis of romantic love. *Neuroreport,* 11 (17), 3829–3834.

Acevedo, B. P., Aron, A., Fisher, H. E., & Brown, L. L. (2011). Neural correlates of long-term intense romantic love. *Social Cognitive and Affective Neuroscience, 7* (2), 145–159.

Kate, P. E., Deshmukh, G. P., Datir, R. P., & Jayraj, R. K. (2017). Good mood foods. *Journal of Nutritional Health and Food Engineering, 7* (4), 345-351.

Hurst, W. J., & Toomey, P. B. (1981). High-performance liquid chromatographic determination of four biogenic amines in chocolate. *Analyst, 106* (1261), 394-402.

Wolfe, D. (2012). *Naked Chocolate: The Astonishing Truth About the World's Greatest Food.* North Atlantic Books.

Jenkins, T. A., Nguyen, J. C., Polglaze, K. E., & Bertrand, P. P. (2016). Influence of tryptophan and serotonin on mood and cognition with a possible role of the gut-brain axis. *Nutrients, 8* (1), 56.

Fink, G. (2016). *Stress: Concepts, Cognition, Emotion, and Behavior: Handbook of Stress Series.* San Diego, CA: Academic Press.

Nestler, E. J., Hyman, S. E., & Malenka, R. C. (2008). *Molecular Neuropharmacology: A Foundation for Clinical Neuroscience, Second Edition.* McGraw Hill Professional.

Weil, B. E. (2005). *Can we cure and forgive adultery?: Staying, not straying: understanding our chemical craving for connection.* West Conshohocken, Pa: Infinity Pub.

Williams, M. J., & Adinoff, B. (2008). The role of acetylcholine in cocaine addiction. *Neuropsychopharmacology: official publication of the American College of Neuropsychopharmacology, 33* (8), 1779–1797.

Calabrò, R. S., Cacciola, A., Bruschetta, D., Milardi, D., Quattrini, F., Sciarrone, F., & Anastasi, G. (2019).

Neuroanatomy and function of human sexual behavior: A neglected or unknown issue?. *Brain and Behavior, 9* (12), e01389.

Langley, L. (2011). *Crazy little thing: How love and sex drive us mad.* Berkeley, Calif: Viva Editions.

Kawabata, H., & Zeki, S. (2008). The neural correlates of desire. *PloS one, 3*(8), e3027.

Roth-Deri, I., Green-Sadan, T., & Yadid, G. (2008). β-Endorphin and drug-induced reward and reinforcement. *Progress in neurobiology, 86* (1), 1-21.

Smyth, P. (2017). *Working with High-Risk Youth: A Relationship-based Practice Framework.* Milton: Taylor and Francis.

van Eimeren, T., Ballanger, B., Pellecchia, G., Miyasaki, J. M., Lang, A. E., & Strafella, A. P. (2009). Dopamine agonists diminish value sensitivity of the orbitofrontal cortex: a trigger for pathological gambling in Parkinson's disease? *Neuropsychopharmacology: Official Publication of the American College of Neuropsychopharmacology, 34* (13), 2758–2766.

Mischel, W., & Ebbesen, E. B. (1970). Attention in delay of gratification. *Journal of Personality and Social Psychology, 16* (2), 329.

Casey, B. J., Somerville, L. H., Gotlib, I. H., Ayduk, O., Franklin, N. T., Askren, M. K., & Glover, G. (2011). Behavioral and neural correlates of delay of gratification 40 years later. *Proceedings of the National Academy of Sciences, 108* (36), 14998-15003.

Perception & Modality

Russell, W. (1974). *The Universal One.* Swannanoa, Waynesboro, Virginia: University of Science and Philosophy.

McMillan, D. W. (2013). *Emotion Rituals: A resource for therapists and clients.* New York: Routledge.

In, I. (2016). *The International Journal of Indian Psychology, Volume 3, Issue 4, No. 65.* Lulu & RED'SHINE Publication. Inc.

Kawabata, H., & Zeki, S. (2008). The neural correlates of desire. *PloS one, 3*(8), e3027.

Roth-Deri, I., Green-Sadan, T., & Yadid, G. (2008). β-Endorphin and drug-induced reward and reinforcement. *Progress in neurobiology, 86* (1), 1-21.

Smyth, P. (2017). *Working with High-Risk Youth: A Relationship-based Practice Framework.* Milton: Taylor and Francis.

van Eimeren, T., Ballanger, B., Pellecchia, G., Miyasaki, J. M., Lang, A. E., & Strafella, A. P. (2009). Dopamine agonists diminish value sensitivity of the orbitofrontal cortex: a trigger for pathological gambling in Parkinson's disease? *Neuropsychopharmacology: Official Publication of the American College of Neuropsychopharmacology, 34* (13), 2758–2766.

Mischel, W., & Ebbesen, E. B. (1970). Attention in delay of gratification. *Journal of Personality and Social Psychology, 16* (2), 329.

Casey, B. J., Somerville, L. H., Gotlib, I. H., Ayduk, O., Franklin, N. T., Askren, M. K., ... & Glover, G. (2011). Behavioral and neural correlates of delay of gratification 40 years later. *Proceedings of the National Academy of Sciences, 108* (36), 14998-15003.

Langley, L. (2011). *Crazy little thing: How love and sex drive us mad.* Berkeley, Calif: Viva Editions.

Acevedo, B. P., Aron, A., Fisher, H. E., & Brown, L. L. (2011). Neural correlates of long-term intense romantic love. *Social Cognitive and Affective Neuroscience,* 7 (2), 145–159.

Fisher, H. E. (1994). *Anatomy of Love: A Natural History of Mating, Marriage, and Why We Stray*. New York: W.W. Norton & Company, Inc.

Fisher, H. (2005). *Why we love: The nature and chemistry of romantic love.* New York: H. Holt.

Chapter 7

Sex

O'Brien, J. (2009). *Encyclopedia of Gender and Society, Volume 1.* London: SAGE.

Weor, S. A. (2012). *The Perfect Matrimony: The Door to Enter Into Initiation: Why Sex and Religion are Inseparable.* Brooklyn, N.Y: Glorian Publishing.

Deveney, J. P. (1997). *Paschal Beverly Randolph: A nineteenth-century Black American spiritualist, rosicrucian, and sex magician.* Albany: State University of New York Press.

Machacek, D. W., & Wilcox, M. M. (2003). *Sexuality and the World's Religions*. Oxford: ABC-CLIO.

Feuerstein, G. (1998). *Tantra: Path of Ecstasy.* Boston: Shambhala Publications.

Urban, H. B. (2012). *Tantra: Sex, Secrecy, Politics, and Power in the Study of Religion.* Delhi: Motilal Banarsidass Publisher.

Wesley, J., & Taylor, J. (1817). *The Doctrine of Original Sin: According to Scripture, Reason, and Experience, in Answer to Dr. Taylor. J.* New York: J. Soule and T. Mason.

Leick, G. (2013). *Sex and Eroticism in Mesopotamian Literature.* Boca Raton, FL: Taylor and Francis, Routledge.

Leeming, D. A. (2010). *Creation Myths of the World: An Encyclopedia. Volume 1.* Calif: ABC-CLIO.

Cross, T. L. F. L., Cross, F. L., & Livingstone, E. A. (2005). *The Oxford Dictionary of the Christian Church.* Oxford University Press.

Initiates, T. (1908). *The Kybalion: A Study of the Hermetic Philosophy of Ancient Egypt and Greece.* Chicago, Illinois: The Yogi Publication Society.

Russell, W. (1994). *The Secret of Light.* Swannanoa, Waynesboro, Virginia: University of Science and Philosophy.

Langley, L. (2011). *Crazy little thing: How love and sex drive us mad.* Berkeley, Calif: Viva Editions.

Laing, R.D. (2010). *The Divided Self: An Existential Study in Sanity and Madness.* Penguin UK.

"And if a kingdom be divided against itself, that kingdom cannot stand."
(Mark 3:24, King James Version).

Samael, A. W. (2013). *The great rebellion: The state of our world and how to change it through practical spirituality*. Brooklyn, N.Y: Glorian.

Samael, A. W. (2007). *The elimination of Satan's tail: Gnostic psychology, meditation, and the origins of suffering*. Aloha, OR: Thelema Press.

Deng, Y., Zhu, S. L., Xu, P., & Deng, H. (2003). Ratio of Qi with modern essential on traditional Chinese medicine Qi: Qi set, Qi element. *J Mathematical Med*, *16*, 346-7.

Etter, C. (2005). *Dyothelemic Christianity*. iUniverse.

Lee, M. S., Pittler, M. H., & Ernst, E. (2008). Effects of reiki in clinical practice: a systematic review of randomised clinical trials. *International Journal of Clinical Practice*, 62 (6), 947–954.

The Orgasm

Robinson, M. (2005, June 23). Why Does A Lover Pull Away after Sex? *REUNITING HEALING WITH SEXUAL RELATIONSHIPS*. Retrieved from https://www.reuniting.info/science/dopamine_separation_after_orgasm

Langley, L. (2011). *Crazy little thing: How love and sex drive us mad*. Berkeley, Calif: Viva Editions.

Fisher, H. (2000). Lust, attraction, attachment: Biology and evolution of the three primary emotion systems for mating, reproduction, and parenting. *Journal of Sex Education and Therapy*, *25* (1), 96-104.

Fisher, H. E., Aron, A., Mashek, D., Li, H., & Brown, L. L. (2002). Defining the brain systems of lust, romantic attraction, and attachment. *Archives of sexual behavior*, *31* (5), 413-419.

Newell, R., & Gournay, K. (2008). *Mental Health Nursing E-Book: An Evidence Based Approach*. London: Elsevier Health Sciences.

Tariri, B. (2013). *Desexed*. Boomington, IN: Author House.

Volkow, N. D., Fowler, J. S., Wang, G. J., Baler, R., & Telang, F. (2008). Imaging dopamine's role in drug abuse and addiction. *Neuropharmacology*, *56 Suppl 1* (Suppl 1), 3–8.

Georgiadis, J. R., & Kringelbach, M. L. (2012). The human sexual response cycle: brain imaging evidence linking sex to other pleasures. *Progress in Neurobiology*, 98 (1), 49–81.

Goodwin, B. C., Browne, M., & Rockloff, M. (2015). Measuring preference for supernormal over natural rewards: a two-dimensional anticipatory pleasure scale. *Evolutionary Psychology*, *13* (4), 1474704915613914.

Kent, M. (2000). *Advanced biology*. Oxford University Press.

Reece, W. O. (2009). *Functional Anatomy and Physiology of Domestic Animals*. New York, NY: John Wiley & Sons.

Gangestad, S. W., & Thornhill, R. (2008). Human oestrus. *Proceedings. Biological sciences*, 275 (1638), 991–1000.

Kruger, T. H. C., Hartmann, U., & Schedlowski, M. (2005). Prolactinergic and dopaminergic mechanisms underlying sexual arousal and orgasm in humans. *World Journal of Urology*, 23 (2), 130–138.

Ben-Jonathan, N., & Hnasko, R. (2001). Dopamine as a prolactin (PRL) inhibitor. *Endocrine Reviews*, 22 (6), 724–763.

Carmichael, M. S., Humbert, R., Dixen, J., Palmisano, G., Greenleaf, W., & Davidson, J. M. (1987). Plasma oxytocin increases in the human sexual response. *The Journal of Clinical Endocrinology and Metabolism*, 64 (1), 27–31.

Hull, E. M., Muschamp, J. W., & Sato, S. (2004). Dopamine and serotonin: influences on male sexual behavior. *Physiology & Behavior*, 83 (2), 291–307.

Will, R. G., Hull, E. M., & Dominguez, J. M. (2014). Influences of dopamine and glutamate in the medial preoptic area on male sexual behavior. *Pharmacology, Biochemistry, and Behavior*, *121*, 115–123.

Robinson, M. Wilson, G. (2006, September 01). Sex and Addiction. *REUNITING HEALING WITH SEXUAL RELATIONSHIPS.* Retrieved from https://www. reuniting.info/science/sex_and_addiction

Contoreggi, C., Herning, R.I., Koeppl, B., Simpson, P.M., Negro, Jr., P.J., Fortner-Burton, C., & Hess, J. (2003). Treatment-seeking inpatient cocaine abusers show hypothalamic dysregulation of both basal prolactin and cortisol secretion. *Neuroendocrinology* 78:154-162

"But of the fruit of the tree which is in the midst of the garden, God hath said, Ye shall not eat of it, neither shall ye touch it, lest ye die." (Genesis 3:3, King James Version).

G, Instructor. (2008, December 17). The Garden of Eden (2). *Kabbalah of Genesis, a Free Online Course.* Retrieved from https://gnosticteachings.org/courses/kabbalah-of-genesis/704-the-garden-of-eden-2.html.

Love, T., Laier, C., Brand, M., Hatch, L., & Hajela, R. (2015). Neuroscience of Internet Pornography Addiction: A Review and Update. *Behavioral sciences (Basel, Switzerland)*, 5 (3), 388-433.

Robinson, M. Wilson, G. (n.d). The Passion Cycle. *REUNITING HEALING WITH SEXUAL RELATIONSHIPS.* Retrieved from https://www.reuniting.info/passion_cycle

Cruz, J.-C., & Reiley, A. (2010). *The Love Diet*. United States: Life of Reiley.

Cacioppo, J. T., Tassinary, L. G., & Berntson, G. (2007). *Handbook of Psychophysiology*. Cambridge: Cambridge University Press.

Johnson, P. M., & Kenny, P. J. (2010). Addiction-like reward dysfunction and compulsive eating in obese rats: Role for dopamine D2 receptors. *Nature neuroscience*, *13* (5), 635.

Kringelbach, M. L., & Berridge, K. C. (2010). The functional neuroanatomy of pleasure and happiness. *Discovery medicine*, *9* (49), 579–587.

Jiang, M., Xin, J., Zou, Q., & Shen, J.-W. (2003). A research on the relationship between ejaculation and serum testosterone level in men. *Journal of Zhejiang University. Science*, 4 (2), 236–240.

Brody, S. (2006). Blood pressure reactivity to stress is better for people who recently had penile-vaginal intercourse than for people who had other or no sexual activity. *Biological Psychology*, 71 (2), 214–222.

Kirby, E. W., Carson, C. C., & Coward, R. M. (2015). Tramadol for the management of premature ejaculation: a timely systematic review. *International Journal Of Impotence Research*, 27, 121.

Sastry, B. V, Janson, V. E., & Owens, L. K. (1991). Significance of substance P- and enkephalin-peptide systems in the male genital tract. *Annals of the New York Academy of Sciences*, *632*, 339–353.

Bancroft, J. (2005). The endocrinology of sexual arousal, *Journal of Endocrinology*, *186* (3), 411-427.

Fernández-Guasti, A., & Rodríguez-Manzo, G. (2003). Pharmacological and physiological aspects of sexual exhaustion in male rats. *Scandinavian journal of psychology*, *44* (3), 257-263.

Carter, C. S. (1992). Oxytocin and sexual behavior. *Neuroscience and Biobehavioral Reviews*, *16* (2), 131—144.

Uvnäs-Moberg, K., Handlin, L., & Petersson, M. (2015). Self-soothing behaviors with particular reference to oxytocin release induced by non-noxious sensory stimulation. *Frontiers in psychology*, *5*, 1529.

Stix, G. (2014). Fact or fiction?: Oxytocin is the 'love hormone'. *Scientific American*, *8*.

Uvnas-Moberg, K., & Petersson, M. (2005). [Oxytocin, a mediator of anti-stress, well-being, social interaction, growth and healing]. *Zeitschrift fur Psychosomatische Medizin und Psychotherapie*, *51* (1), 57–80.

Mirin, S. M., Meyer, R. E., Mendelson, J. H., & Ellingboe, J. (1980). Opiate use and sexual function. *The American Journal of Psychiatry*, *137* (8), 909–915.

Lindow, S. W., Spuy, Z. M., Hendricks, M. S., Rosselli, A. P., Lombard, C., & Leng, G. (1992). The effect of morphine and naloxone administration on plasma oxytocin concentrations in the first stage of labour. *Clinical Endocrinology*, *37* (4), 349–353.

Exton, M. S., Kruger, T. H., Koch, M., Paulson, E., Knapp, W., Hartmann, U., & Schedlowski, M. (2001). Coitus-induced orgasm stimulates prolactin secretion in healthy subjects. *Psychoneuroendocrinology*, *26*, 287–294.

Kennett, J. E., & McKee, D. T. (2012). Oxytocin: an emerging regulator of prolactin secretion in the female rat. *Journal of neuroendocrinology*, *24* (3), 403-412.

Kruger, T. H. C., Haake, P., Chereath, D., Knapp, W., Janssen, O. E., Exton, M. S., & Hartmann, U. (2003). Specificity of the neuroendocrine response to orgasm during sexual arousal in men. *Journal of Endocrinology, 177* (1), 57.

Magon, N., & Kalra, S. (2011). The orgasmic history of oxytocin: Love, lust, and labor. *Indian journal of endocrinology and metabolism, 15 Suppl 3* (Suppl3), S156–S161.

Esch, T., & Stefano, G. B. (2005). The neurobiology of love. *Neuroendocrinology Letters, 26* (3), 175-192.

Jansen, A. S., Van Nguyen, X., Karpitskiy, V., Mettenleiter, T. C., & Loewy, A. D. (1995). Central command neurons of the sympathetic nervous system: basis of the fight-or-flight response. *Science, 270* (5236), 644-646.

Meston, C. M., & Gorzalka, B. B. (1992). Psychoactive Drugs and Human Sexual Behavior: The Role of Serotonergic Activity. *Journal of Psychoactive Drugs, 24* (1), 1–40.

Zajecka, J., Fawcett, J., Schaff, M., Jeffriess, H., & Guy, C. (1991). The role of serotonin in sexual dysfunction: Fluoxetine-associated orgasm dysfunction. *The Journal of Clinical Psychiatry*, Vol. 52, pp. 66–68. US: Physicians Postgraduate Press.

Fuller, R. W., & Clemens, J. A. (1981). Role of serotonin in the hypothalamic regulation of pituitary function. In *Serotonin* (pp. 431-444). Springer, Boston, MA.

Giustina, A., & Braunstein, G. D. (2016). "Hypothalamic syndromes," in *Endocrinology: Adult and Pediatric,* eds J. L. Jameson, L. J. De Groot, D. de Kretser, L. C. Giudice, A. Grossman, S. Melmed, J. T. Potts Jr, and G. C. Weir (Philadelphia, PA: Elsevier), 174-187.e5.

Pickardt, C. R., & Scriba, P. C. (1985). TRH: Pathophysiologic and clinical implications. *Acta Neurochirurgica*, 75 (1), 43–48.

Kanasaki, H., Oride, A., Mijiddorj, T., & Kyo, S. (2015). Role of thyrotropin-releasing hormone in prolactin-producing cell models. *Neuropeptides, 54,* 73-77.

Molitch, M. E. (2009). Prolactin in human reproduction. In *Yen & Jaffe's Reproductive Endocrinology* (pp. 57-78). Elsevier Inc.

Calabrò, R. S., Cacciola, A., Bruschetta, D., Milardi, D., Quattrini, F., Sciarrone, F., & Anastasi, G. (2019). Neuroanatomy and function of human sexual behavior: A neglected or unknown issue? *Brain and Behavior, 9* (12), e01389.

Wolfe, D. (2012). *Naked Chocolate: The Astonishing Truth About the World's Greatest Food.* North Atlantic Books.

Rastrelli G, Corona G, Maggi M (2018). "Testosterone and sexual function in men". *Maturitas*. 112: 46–52.

Schacter, D., Gilbert, D., Wegner, D., & Hood, B. (2015). *Psychology: Second European Edition*. Macmillan International Higher Education.

Fletcher, G. J. O. (2019). *The science of intimate relationships. Newark,* N.J: Wiley Blackwell.

Emilien, G. (2002). *Anxiety disorders: Pathophysiology and pharmacological treatment*. Basel: Birkhäuser.

Zeitlin, S. I., & Rajfer, J. (2000). Hyperprolactinemia and erectile dysfunction. *Reviews in urology, 2* (1), 39–42.

Grattan D. R. (2015). 60 YEARS OF NEUROENDOCRINOLOGY: The hypothalamo-prolactin axis. *The Journal of endocrinology, 226* (2), T101–T122.

Warnock, J. K., Swanson, S. G., Borel, R. W., Zipfel, L. M., Brennan, J. J., & ESTRATEST Clinical Study Group. (2005). Combined esterified estrogens and methyltestosterone versus esterified estrogens alone in the treatment of loss of sexual interest in surgically menopausal women. *Menopause, 12* (4), 374-384.

Heiman, J. R., Rupp, H., Janssen, E., Newhouse, S. K., Brauer, M., & Laan, E. (2011). Sexual desire, sexual arousal and hormonal differences in premenopausal US and Dutch women with and without low sexual desire. *Hormones and behavior, 59* (5), 772-779.

Larsen, C. M., & Grattan, D. R. (2012). Prolactin, neurogenesis, and maternal behaviors. *Brain, Behavior, and Immunity, 26* (2), 201–209.

Hiller, J. (2005). Gender differences in sexual motivation. *The journal of men's health & gender, 2* (3), 339-345.

Keil, M., Wetterauer, U., & Heite, H. J. (1979). Glutamic acid concentration in human semen--its origin and significance. *Andrologia, 11* (5), 385–391.

Dominguez, J. M., Gil, M., & Hull, E. M. (2006). Preoptic glutamate facilitates male sexual behavior. *Journal of Neuroscience, 26* (6), 1699-1703.

Wu, L. J., Kim, S. S., Li, X., Zhang, F., & Zhuo, M. (2009). Sexual attraction enhances glutamate transmission in mammalian anterior cingulate cortex. *Molecular brain, 2*, 9.

Moore, K. M., Oelberg, W. L., Glass, M. R., Johnson, M. D., Been, L. E., & Meisel, R. L. (2019). Glutamate afferents from the medial prefrontal cortex mediate nucleus accumbens activation by female sexual behavior. *Frontiers in behavioral neuroscience, 13*, 227.

Perception & Modality

Initiates, T. (1908). *The Kybalion: A Study of the Hermetic Philosophy of Ancient Egypt and Greece*. Chicago, Illinois: The Yogi Publication Society.

Samael, A. W. (2013). *The Great Rebellion: The state of our world and how to change it through practical spirituality*. Brooklyn, N.Y: Glorian.

Volkow, N. D., Fowler, J. S., Wang, G. J., Baler, R., & Telang, F. (2008). Imaging dopamine's role in drug abuse and addiction. *Neuropharmacology, 56 Suppl 1* (Suppl 1), 3–8.

Georgiadis, J. R., & Kringelbach, M. L. (2012). The human sexual response cycle: brain imaging evidence linking sex to other pleasures. *Progress in Neurobiology*, 98 (1), 49–81.

Langley, L. (2011). *Crazy little thing: How love and sex drive us mad*. Berkeley, Calif: Viva Editions.

Kruger, T. H. C., Hartmann, U., & Schedlowski, M. (2005). Prolactinergic and dopaminergic mechanisms underlying sexual arousal and orgasm in humans. *World Journal of Urology*, 23 (2), 130–138.

Kruger, T. H. C., Haake, P., Chereath, D., Knapp, W., Janssen, O. E., Exton, M. S., & Hartmann, U. (2003). Specificity of the neuroendocrine response to orgasm during sexual arousal in men. *Journal of Endocrinology*, *177* (1), 57.

Magon, N., & Kalra, S. (2011). The orgasmic history of oxytocin: Love, lust, and labor. *Indian journal of endocrinology and metabolism*, *15 Suppl 3* (Suppl3), S156–S161.

Esch, T., & Stefano, G. B. (2005). The neurobiology of love. *Neuroendocrinology Letters*, *26* (3), 175-192.

Russell, W. (1994). *The Secret of Light*. Swannanoa, Waynesboro, Virginia: University of Science and Philosophy.

Weor, S. A. (2013). *Beyond Death*. Glorian Publishing.

"For what shall it profit a man, if he shall gain the whole world, and lose his own soul?" (Mark 8:36, King James Version).

Fisher, H. (2000). Lust, attraction, attachment: Biology and evolution of the three primary emotion systems for mating, reproduction, and parenting. *Journal of Sex Education and Therapy*, *25* (1), 96-104.

Gonzalez-Wippler, Migene (1991). *Complete Book Of Amulets & Talismans*. St. Paul, MN: Llewellyn Worldwide.

Fisher, H. E., Aron, A., Mashek, D., Li, H., & Brown, L. L. (2002). Defining the brain systems of lust, romantic attraction, and attachment. *Archives of sexual behavior*, *31*(5), 413-419.

G, Instructor. (2008, October 06). The Garden of Eden (3). *Kabbalah of Genesis, a Free Online Course*. Retrieved from https://gnosticteachings.org/courses/kabbalah-of-genesis/693-the-garden-of-eden-3.html

Emoto, M., & Thayne, D. A. (2011). *The Hidden Messages in Water*. New York: Atria Books.

Stroebe, W., Papies, E. K., & Aarts, H. (2008). From Homeostatic to Hedonic Theories of Eating: Self-Regulatory Failure in Food-Rich Environments. *Applied Psychology*, 57 (s1), 172–193.

Chapter 8

Love

Russell, W. (1974). *The Universal One.* Swannanoa, Waynesboro, Virginia: University of Science and Philosophy.

Fisher, H. (2000). Lust, attraction, attachment: Biology and evolution of the three primary emotion systems for mating, reproduction, and parenting. *Journal of Sex Education and Therapy*, *25* (1), 96-104.

Fisher, H. E., Aron, A., Mashek, D., Li, H., & Brown, L. L. (2002). Defining the brain systems of lust, romantic attraction, and attachment. *Archives of sexual behavior, 31* (5), 413-419.

Fisher, H. E. (1992). *Anatomy of love: A natural history of mating, marriage, and why we stray*. New York: Fawcett Columbine.

Martinich, A. P., & Hobbes, T. (1998). *A Hobbes dictionary*. Malden, Mass: Blackwell.

Gere, C. (2017). *Pain, pleasure, and the greater good: From the Panopticon to the Skinner box and beyond*. Chicago, Illinois; London, England: The University of Chicago Press.

Hobbes, T., & Molesworth, W. (1839). *The English works of Thomas Hobbes of Malmesbury*. London: J. Bohn.

Inagaki, T., & I Eisenberger, N. (2013). Shared Neural Mechanisms Underlying Social Warmth and Physical Warmth. In *Psychological science* (Vol. 24).

Williams, L. E., & Bargh, J. A. (2008). Experiencing physical warmth promotes interpersonal warmth. *Science (New York, N.Y.), 322* (5901), 606–607.

Tashi, T., & McDougall, G. (2010). *Relative truth, ultimate truth*. Surry Hills, NSW: Read How You Want.

Park, S. (1983). *Buddhist Faith and Sudden Enlightenment*. New York: SUNY Press.

Cozort, D., & Shields, J. M. (2018). *The Oxford Handbook of Buddhist Ethics*. Oxford: Oxford University Press.

Bonnes, M., Lee, T., & Bonaiuto, M. (2003). *Psychological Theories for Environmental Issues*. Aldershot: Ashgate.

Gottlieb, R. S. (2013). *Spirituality: What it is and why it matters*. New York: Oxford University Press.

Benedict XVI. P. (2009). *Charity in truth*. San Francisco: Ignatius Press.

Chen, C., Crivelli, C., Garrod, O. G., Schyns, P. G., Fernández-Dols, J. M., & Jack, R. E. (2018). Distinct facial expressions represent pain and pleasure across cultures. *Proceedings of the National Academy of Sciences, 115* (43), E10013-E10021.

Tamam, S., & Ahmad, A. H. (2017). Love as a Modulator of Pain. *The Malaysian journal of medical sciences: MJMS, 24* (3), 5–14.

Fisher, H. (2005). *Why we love: The nature and chemistry of romantic love*. New York: H. Holt.

Arnold, M. B. (1972). *Feelings and emotions: The Loyola symposium*. New York: Academic Press.

Miller, J. G., Kahle, S., Lopez, M., & Hastings, P. D. (2015). Compassionate love buffers stress-reactive mothers from fight-or-flight parenting. *Developmental psychology, 51* (1), 36.

Müller, M. S., Vyssotski, A. L., Yamamoto, M., & Yoda, K. (2017). Heart rate variability reveals that a decrease in parasympathetic ('rest-and-digest') activity dominates autonomic stress responses in a free-living seabird. *Comparative Biochemistry and Physiology Part A: Molecular & Integrative Physiology, 212*, 117-126.

Adameyko, I., & Ernfors, P. (2014). Nerves transport stem-like cells generating parasympathetic neurons. *Cell Cycle, 13* (18), 2805-2806.

Adameyko, I. (2016). Neural circuitry gets rewired. *Science, 354* (6314), 833-834.

Stover, S. A. (2011). *The way of the happy woman: Living the best year of your life*. Novato, Calif: New World Library.

McMillan, D. W. (2013). *Emotion Rituals: A resource for therapists and clients*. New York: Routledge.

Levey, M., & Library, 1st world. (2004). *The Book of the Holy Light*. 1st World Publishing, Incorporated.

Puglisi-Allegra, S., & Andolina, D. (2015). Serotonin and stress coping. *Behavioural Brain Research, 277*, 58–67.

Fisher, H. E., Aron, A., & Brown, L. L. (2006). Romantic love: a mammalian brain system for mate choice. *Philosophical transactions of the Royal Society of London. Series B, Biological sciences, 361* (1476), 2173–2186.

Stix, G. (2014). Fact or fiction?: Oxytocin is the 'love hormone'. *Scientific American, 8*.

Uvnas-Moberg, K., & Petersson, M. (2005). [Oxytocin, a mediator of anti-stress, well-being, social interaction, growth and healing]. *Zeitschrift fur Psychosomatische Medizin und Psychotherapie, 51* (1), 57–80.

Sabelli, H. C., & Javaid, J. I. (1995). Phenylethylamine modulation of affect: therapeutic and diagnostic implications. *The Journal of Neuropsychiatry and Clinical Neurosciences, 7* (1), 6–14.

Fischer, A. G., & Ullsperger, M. (2017). An Update on the Role of Serotonin and its Interplay with Dopamine for Reward. *Frontiers in human neuroscience*, 11, 484.

Nestler, E. J., Hyman, S. E., & Malenka, R. C. (2008). *Molecular Neuropharmacology: A Foundation for Clinical Neuroscience, Second Edition*. McGraw Hill Professional.

Langley, L. (2011). *Crazy little thing: How love and sex drive us mad*. Berkeley, Calif: Viva Editions.

Samardzic, J., Jadzic, D., Hencic, B., Jancic, J., & Strac, D. S. (2018). Introductory Chapter: GABA/Glutamate Balance: A Key for Normal Brain Functioning. GABA And Glutamate: *New Developments In Neurotransmission Research*, 1.

Lydiard, R. B. (2003). The role of GABA in anxiety disorders. *The Journal of clinical psychiatry, 64*, 21-27.

Abdou, A. M., Higashiguchi, S., Horie, K., Kim, M., Hatta, H., & Yokogoshi, H. (2006). Relaxation and immunity enhancement effects of γ-Aminobutyric acid (GABA) administration in humans. *Biofactors*, *26* (3), 201-208.

McCorry, L. K. (2007). Physiology of the autonomic nervous system. *American Journal of Pharmaceutical Education*, *71* (4), 78.

Taylor, S. E., Klein, L. C., Lewis, B. P., Gruenewald, T. L., Gurung, R. A., & Updegraff, J. A. (2000). Biobehavioral responses to stress in females: tend-and-befriend, not fight-or-flight. *Psychological Review*, *107* (3), 411–429.

Jansen, A. S., Nguyen, X. V, Karpitskiy, V., Mettenleiter, T. C., & Loewy, A. D. (1995). Central command neurons of the sympathetic nervous system: basis of the fight-or-flight response. *Science (New York, N.Y.)*, *270* (5236), 644–646.

Childs, G. (1995). *Understand your temperament*. London: Sophia.

Eysenck, H. J. (1967). *The biological basis of personality*. Springfield, Ill: C.C. Thomas.

Ekstrand, D. W. (2018, September 25). *THE FOUR HUMAN TEMPERAMENTS*. Retrieved fromhttp://www. thetransformedsoul.com/additional-studies/miscellaneous-studies/the-four-human-temperaments.

Richard, S. (2017). *Lead Like a Superhero: What Pop Culture Icons Can Teach Us About Impactful Leadership.* Morgan James Publishing.

Neurochemistry & Physiology

Fisher, H. E., Aron, A., & Brown, L. L. (2006). Romantic love: a mammalian brain system for mate choice. *Philosophical transactions of the Royal Society of London. Series B, Biological sciences*, *361* (1476), 2173–2186.

Fisher, H. (2005). *Why we love: The nature and chemistry of romantic love*. New York: H. Holt.

Fisher, H. (2000). Lust, attraction, attachment: Biology and evolution of the three primary emotion systems for mating, reproduction, and parenting. *Journal of Sex Education and Therapy*, *25* (1), 96-104.

Fisher, H. E., Aron, A., Mashek, D., Li, H., & Brown, L. L. (2002). Defining the brain systems of lust, romantic attraction, and attachment. *Archives of sexual behavior*, *31* (5), 413-419.

Fisher, H. E. (1992). *Anatomy of love: A natural history of mating, marriage, and why we stray*. New York: Fawcett Columbine.

Maryam, S., & Bhatia, M. S. (2009). Love and mental health. *Delhi Psychiatry J*, *12* (2), 206-12.

MacDonald, M. (2008). *Your brain: The missing manual: how to get the most from your mind*. Sebastopol, CA: Pogue Press/O'Reilly.

Arnold, M. B. (1972). *Feelings and emotions: The Loyola symposium*. New York: Academic Press.

Miller, J. G., Kahle, S., Lopez, M., & Hastings, P. D. (2015). Compassionate love buffers stress-reactive mothers from fight-or-flight parenting. *Developmental psychology*, *51* (1), 36.

Müller, M. S., Vyssotski, A. L., Yamamoto, M., & Yoda, K. (2017). Heart rate variability reveals that a decrease in parasympathetic ('rest-and-digest') activity dominates autonomic stress responses in a free-living seabird. *Comparative Biochemistry and Physiology Part A: Molecular & Integrative Physiology*, 212, 117-126.

Adameyko, I., & Ernfors, P. (2014). Nerves transport stem-like cells generating parasympathetic neurons. *Cell Cycle*, *13* (18), 2805-2806.

Adameyko, I. (2016). Neural circuitry gets rewired. *Science*, *354* (6314), 833-834.

Goleman, D. (1995). *Emotional Intelligence*. London: Bantam Books.

Bamba, P. A. (2010). *Perfect marriage, not a mirage: A journey through ups and downs of marriage*. New Delhi: Pustak Mahal.

Wolfe, D. (2012). *Naked Chocolate: The Astonishing Truth About the World's Greatest Food*. North Atlantic Books.

Crooks, R. L., & Baur, K. (2010). *Our Sexuality*. Belmont, CA: Wadsworth, Cengage Learning.

Wu, L. J., Kim, S. S., Li, X., Zhang, F., & Zhuo, M. (2009). Sexual attraction enhances glutamate transmission in mammalian anterior cingulate cortex. *Molecular brain*, *2*, 9.

Moore, K. M., Oelberg, W. L., Glass, M. R., Johnson, M. D., Been, L. E., & Meisel, R. L. (2019). Glutamate afferents from the medial prefrontal cortex mediate nucleus accumbens activation by female sexual behavior. *Frontiers in behavioral neuroscience*, *13*, 227.

Dominguez, J. M., Gil, M., & Hull, E. M. (2006). Preoptic glutamate facilitates male sexual behavior. *Journal of Neuroscience*, *26* (6), 1699-1703.

Fisher, H. (2000). Lust, attraction, attachment: Biology and evolution of the three primary emotion systems for mating, reproduction, and parenting. In *Journal of Sex Education and Therapy* (Vol. 25).

Fadul, J. A. (2014). *Encyclopedia of theory & practice in psychotherapy & counseling*. Raleigh, NC: Lulu Press.

Seshadri K. G. (2016). The neuroendocrinology of love. *Indian journal of endocrinology and metabolism*, *20* (4), 558–563.

Husband, T. (2016). *The chemistry of human nature*. Cambridge: Royal Society of Chemistry.

Sfetcu, N. (2014). *Dating and Interpersonal Relationships*. Nicolae Sfetcu.

Taylor, S. E., Klein, L. C., Lewis, B. P., Gruenewald, T. L., Gurung, R. A., & Updegraff, J. A. (2000). Biobehavioral responses to stress in females: tend-and-befriend, not fight-or-flight. *Psychological review*, *107* (3), 411.

Uvnäs-Moberg, K., Handlin, L., & Petersson, M. (2015). Self-soothing behaviors with particular reference to oxytocin release induced by non-noxious sensory stimulation. *Frontiers in psychology, 5*, 1529.

Uvnas-Moberg, K., & Petersson, M. (2005). [Oxytocin, a mediator of anti-stress, well-being, social interaction, growth and healing]. *Zeitschrift fur Psychosomatische Medizin und Psychotherapie, 51* (1), 57–80.

Sohal, V. S. (2013). Serotonin Gives Oxytocin a Helping Hand. *Science Translational Medicine, 5* (207), 207ec172--207ec172.

Dayton, T. (2007). *Emotional Sobriety: From Relationship Trauma to Resilience and Balance.* Health Communications, Inc.

Love T. M. (2014). Oxytocin, motivation and the role of dopamine. *Pharmacology, biochemistry, and behavior, 119*, 49–60.

Colonnello, V., & Heinrichs, M. (2016). Oxytocin and Self-Consciousness. *Frontiers in human neuroscience, 10*, 67.

Magon, N., & Kalra, S. (2011). The orgasmic history of oxytocin: Love, lust, and labor. *Indian journal of endocrinology and metabolism, 15 Suppl 3* (Suppl3), S156-61.

R. Murphy, M., R. Seckl, J., Burton, S., A. Checkley, S., & Lightman, S. (1987). Changes In Oxytocin and Vasopressin Secretion During Sexual Activity in Men. *The Journal of Clinical Endocrinology and Metabolism, 65*, 738–741.

Comas-Diaz, L., & Weiner, M. B. (2016). *Women Psychotherapists' Reflections on Female Friendships: Sisters of the Heart.* Routledge.

Heinrichs, M., Baumgartner, T., Kirschbaum, C., & Ehlert, U. (2003). Social support and oxytocin interact to suppress cortisol and subjective responses to psychosocial stress. *Biological Psychiatry, 54* (12), 1389–1398.

Harmon-Jones, E., & Winkielman, P. (2007). *Social Neuroscience: Integrating Biological and Psychological Explanations of Social Behavior.* Guilford Publications.

Bushko, R. G. (2009). *Strategy for the Future of Health.* IOS Press.

Goleman, D. (1995). *Emotional Intelligence.* Bantam Books.

Bartels, A., & Zeki, S. (2000). The neural basis of romantic love. *Neuroreport, 11* (17), 3829–3834.

Tancredi, L. (2005). *Hardwired Behavior: What Neuroscience Reveals about Morality.* Cambridge: Cambridge University Press.

Mayer E. A. (2011). Gut feelings: the emerging biology of gut-brain communication. *Nature reviews. Neuroscience, 12* (8), 453–466.

Phan, K. L., Wager, T., Taylor, S. F., & Liberzon, I. (2002). Functional neuroanatomy of emotion: a meta-analysis of emotion activation studies in PET and fMRI. *NeuroImage, 16* (2), 331–348.

Oppenheimer, S. M., Gelb, A., Girvin, J. P., & Hachinski, V. C. (1992). Cardiovascular effects of human insular cortex stimulation. *Neurology, 42* (9), 1727–1732.

Fink, G. R., Frackowiak, R. S. J., Pietrzyk, U., & Passingham, R. E. (1997). Multiple Nonprimary Motor Areas in the Human Cortex. *Journal of Neurophysiology, 77* (4), 2164–2174.

Craig, A. D. (2009). How do you feel - now? The anterior insula and human awareness. *Nature Reviews Neuroscience, 10*, 59.

Bushara, K. O., Grafman, J., & Hallett, M. (2001). Neural Correlates of Auditory-Visual Stimulus Onset Asynchrony Detection. *Journal of Neuroscience, 21* (1), 300–304.

Craig, A. D. (2003). A new view of pain as a homeostatic emotion. *Trends in Neurosciences, 26* (6), 303–307.

Ramírez-Amaya, V., & Bermudez-Rattoni, F. (1999). Conditioned Enhancement of Antibody Production Is Disrupted by Insular Cortex and Amygdala but Not Hippocampal Lesions. *Brain, Behavior, and Immunity, 13* (1), 46–60.

Phan, K. L., Wager, T., Taylor, S. F., & Liberzon, I. (2002). Functional neuroanatomy of emotion: a meta-analysis of emotion activation studies in PET and fMRI. *NeuroImage, 16* (2), 331–348.

Sanfey, A. G., Rilling, J. K., Aronson, J. A., Nystrom, L. E., & Cohen, J. D. (2003). The Neural Basis of Economic Decision-Making in the Ultimatum Game. *Science, 300* (5626), 1755–1758.

Paulus, M. P., & Stein, M. B. (2006). An Insular View of Anxiety. *Biological Psychiatry, 60* (4), 383–387.

Singer, T. (2006). The neuronal basis and ontogeny of empathy and mind reading: review of literature and implications for future research. *Neurosci Biobehav Rev*. 30 (6): 855–63.

Ortigue, S., Grafton, S. T., & Bianchi-Demicheli, F. (2007). Correlation between insula activation and self-reported quality of orgasm in women. *NeuroImage, 37* (2), 551–560.

Belfi, A. M., Koscik, T. R., & Tranel, D. (2015). Damage to the insula is associated with abnormal interpersonal trust. *Neuropsychologia, 71*, 165–172.

Baliki, M. N., Geha, P. Y., & Apkarian, A. V. (2009). Parsing pain perception between nociceptive representation and magnitude estimation. *Journal of Neurophysiology, 101* (2), 875–887.

Ogino, Y., Nemoto, H., Inui, K., Saito, S., Kakigi, R., & Goto, F. (2006). Inner Experience of Pain: Imagination of Pain While Viewing Images Showing Painful Events Forms Subjective Pain Representation in Human Brain. *Cerebral Cortex, 17* (5), 1139–1146.

Aziz-Zadeh, L., & Damasio, A. (2008). Embodied semantics for actions: Findings from functional brain imaging. *Journal of Physiology-Paris, 102* (1), 35–39.

Dalgleish, T. (2004). The emotional brain. *Nature Reviews Neuroscience*. 5 (7): 582–89.

Olausson, H., Charron, J., Marchand, S., Villemure, C., Strigo, I. A., & Bushnell, M. C. (2005). Feelings of warmth correlate with neural activity in right anterior insular cortex. *Neuroscience Letters, 389* (1), 1–5.

Inagaki, T., & I Eisenberger, N. (2013). Shared Neural Mechanisms Underlying Social Warmth and Physical Warmth. In *Psychological science* (Vol. 24).

Williams, L. E., & Bargh, J. A. (2008). Experiencing physical warmth promotes interpersonal warmth. *Science (New York, N.Y.), 322* (5901), 606–607.

Craig, A. D. (2011). Significance of the insula for the evolution of human awareness of feelings from the body. *Annals of the New York Academy of Sciences, 1225* (1), 72–82.

McRae, K., Misra, S., Prasad, A. K., Pereira, S. C., & Gross, J. J. (2012). Bottom-up and top-down emotion generation: implications for emotion regulation. *Social cognitive and affective neuroscience, 7* (3), 253–262.

Lydiard, R. B. (2003). The role of GABA in anxiety disorders. *The Journal of Clinical Psychiatry, 64 Suppl 3*, 21–27.

Liebowitz, M. R. (1984). *The Chemistry of Love*. New York: Berkley Books.

Fisher, H. (1994). The nature of romantic love. *Journal of NIH Research, 6* (4).

Patil, Y. (2014). The Chemistry of Love. *International Journal of Scientific & Engineering Research, 5* (4), 1317-1319.

Chaudhry, S. R., & Bhimji, S. S. (2018). Biochemistry, Endorphin. In *StatPearls [Internet]*. StatPearls Publishing.

Amir, S., Brown, Z. W., & Amit, Z. (1980). The role of endorphins in stress: Evidence and speculations. *Neuroscience & Biobehavioral Reviews, 4* (1), 77–86.

Khajehei, M., & Behroozpour, E. (2018). Endorphins, oxytocin, sexuality and romantic relationships. *World J Obstet Gynecol, 7* (2), 17-23.

Craig, A. D., Chen, K., Bandy, D., & Reiman, E. M. (2000). Thermosensory activation of insular cortex. *Nature Neuroscience, 3* (2), 184–190.

Phan, K. L., Wager, T., Taylor, S. F., & Liberzon, I. (2002). Functional neuroanatomy of emotion: a meta-analysis of emotion activation studies in PET and fMRI. *NeuroImage, 16* (2), 331–348.

Williams, L. E., & Bargh, J. A. (2008). Experiencing physical warmth promotes interpersonal warmth. *Science (New York, N.Y.), 322* (5901), 606-7.

Perception & Modality

Fisher, H. (2005). *Why we love: The nature and chemistry of romantic love*. New York: H. Holt.

Fisher, H. (2000). Lust, attraction, attachment: Biology and evolution of the three primary emotion systems for mating, reproduction, and parenting. *Journal of Sex Education and Therapy, 25* (1), 96-104.

Fisher, H. E., Aron, A., Mashek, D., Li, H., & Brown, L. L. (2002). Defining the brain systems of lust, romantic attraction, and attachment. *Archives of sexual behavior, 31* (5), 413-419.

Fisher, H. E. (1992). *Anatomy of love: A natural history of mating, marriage, and why we stray.* New York: Fawcett Columbine.

Russell, W. (1994). *The Secret of Light.* Swannanoa, Waynesboro, Virginia: University of Science and Philosophy.

Russell, W. (1974). *The Universal One.* Swannanoa, Waynesboro, Virginia: University of Science and Philosophy.

Davies, G. E., & Soundy, T. J. (2009). The genetics of smoking and nicotine addiction. *South Dakota Medicine.*

Maslow, A., & Lewis, K. J. (1987). Maslow's hierarchy of needs. *Salenger Incorporated, 14,* 987.

Schulkin, J., & Schulkin, R. P. P. B. J. (2004). *Allostasis, Homeostasis, and the Costs of Physiological Adaptation.* Cambridge: Cambridge University Press.

Nutt, D. J. (2008). Relationship of neurotransmitters to the symptoms of major depressive disorder. *The Journal of clinical psychiatry, 69,* 4-7.

Kraus, M. W., & Park, J. W. (2014). The undervalued self: Social class and self-evaluation. *Frontiers in psychology, 5,* 1404.

Kross, E., Berman, M. G., Mischel, W., Smith, E. E., & Wager, T. D. (2011). Social rejection shares somatosensory representations with physical pain. *Proceedings of the National Academy of Sciences, 108* (15), 6270-6275.

Cheng, Y., Chen, C., Lin, C. P., Chou, K. H., & Decety, J. (2010). Love hurts: an fMRI study. *Neuroimage, 51* (2), 923-929.

Braden, G. (1997). *Walking between the worlds: The science of compassion.* Bellevue, Wash: Radio Bookstore Press.

Levey, M., & Library, 1stworld. (2004). *The Book of the Holy Light.* Fairfield, IA: 1st World Publishing, Incorporated.

Chapter 9

Pain

Bolger, E. (1999). Grounded theory analysis of emotional pain. *Psychotherapy Research, 9* (3), 342-362.

MacDonald, G., & Leary, M. R. (2005). Why does social exclusion hurt? The relationship between social and physical pain. *Psychological bulletin, 131*(2), 202.

Merskey, H., Bogduk, N., & for the Study of Pain. Task Force on Taxonomy, I. A. (1994). *Classification of Chronic Pain: Descriptions of Chronic Pain Syndromes and Definitions of Pain Terms*. IASP Press.

Fink, G. (2016). *Stress: Concepts, Cognition, Emotion, and Behavior: Handbook of Stress Series*. San Diego, CA: Academic Press.

Cannon, W.B. (1932). *The Wisdom of the Body*. W.W. New York: Norton.

Hobbes, T., & Molesworth, W. (1839). *The English works of Thomas Hobbes of Malmesbury*. London: J. Bohn.

Russell, W. (1974). *The Universal One*. Swannanoa, Waynesboro, Virginia: University of Science and Philosophy.

Lumley, M. A., Cohen, J. L., Borszcz, G. S., Cano, A., Radcliffe, A. M., Porter, L. S., Keefe, F. J. (2011). Pain and emotion: a biopsychosocial review of recent research. *Journal of clinical psychology, 67* (9), 942–968.

McMillan, D. W. (2013). *Emotion Rituals: A resource for therapists and clients*. New York: Routledge.

Puglisi-Allegra, S., & Andolina, D. (2015). Serotonin and stress coping. *Behavioural Brain Research, 277,* 58–67.

Nestler, E. J., Hyman, S. E., & Malenka, R. C. (2008). *Molecular Neuropharmacology: A Foundation for Clinical Neuroscience, Second Edition*. New York: McGraw Hill Professional.

Langley, L. (2011). *Crazy little thing: How love and sex drive us mad*. Berkeley, Calif: Viva Editions.

Watanabe, M., Maemura, K., Kanbara, K., Tamayama, T., & Hayasaki, H. (2002). GABA and GABA receptors in the central nervous system and other organs. *International Review of Cytology, 213,* 1–47.

Garland, E. L. (2012). Pain processing in the human nervous system: a selective review of nociceptive and biobehavioral pathways. *Primary care, 39* (3), 561–571.

Tamam, S., & Ahmad, A. H. (2017). Love as a Modulator of Pain. *The Malaysian journal of medical sciences: MJMS, 24* (3), 5–14.

Chen, C., Crivelli, C., Garrod, O. G., Schyns, P. G., Fernández-Dols, J. M., & Jack, R. E. (2018). Distinct facial expressions represent pain and pleasure across cultures. *Proceedings of the National Academy of Sciences, 115* (43), E10013-E10021.

Mruk, C. J., & Hartzell, J. (2006). *Zen and psychotherapy: Integrating traditional and nontraditional approaches*. New York: Springer Publishing Company.

McMillan, D. W. (2013). *Emotion Rituals: A resource for therapists and clients*. New York: Routledge.

Blevins, W. L. (2014). *Hidden Grace: Growing Through Loss and Grief*. Bloomington, IN: Balboa Press.

Michaelson, S. (2004). *Love Smart: Transforming the Emotional Patterns that Sabotage Relationships*. PA: Prospect Books.

Whitehead, E. E., & Whitehead, J. D. (2010). *Transforming our painful emotions: Spiritual resources in anger, shame, grief, fear, and loneliness*. Maryknoll, N.Y: Orbis Books.

Leary M. R. (2015). Emotional responses to interpersonal rejection. *Dialogues in clinical neuroscience, 17* (4), 435–441.

Weor, S. A. (2012). *The Perfect Matrimony: The Door to Enter Into Initiation: Why Sex and Religion are Inseparable*. Brooklyn, N.Y: Glorian Publishing.

Wisdoms Friend. (n.d). Death and Darkness, Life and Light: The Separation. *Christian-Faith*. Retrieved from https://www.christian-faith.com/death-and-darkness-life-and-light-the-separation/

Greene, L., & Hand, R. (2011). *Saturn: A new look at an old devil*. San Francisco, Calif: Weiser Books.

Macey, S. L. (2013). *Encyclopedia of Time. In Garland Reference Library of Social Science*. New York: Routledge.

Pike, A. (1871). *Morals and Dogma of the Ancient and Accepted Scottish Rite of Freemasonry*. Mansfield Centre, CT: Martino Pub.

Abel, E. L. (2009). *Death Gods: An Encyclopedia of the Rulers, Evil Spirits, and Geographies of the Dead*. Westport, Conn: Greenwood Press.

Neurochemistry & Physiology

Garland, E. L. (2012). Pain processing in the human nervous system: a selective review of nociceptive and biobehavioral pathways. *Primary care, 39* (3), 561–571.

Contrada, R., & Baum, A. (2010). *The Handbook of Stress Science: Biology, Psychology, and Health*. New York: Springer Publishing Company.

McCorry, L. K. (2007). Physiology of the autonomic nervous system. *American Journal of Pharmaceutical Education, 71* (4), 78.

Eisenberger, N. I., & Lieberman, M. D. (2005). Why It Hurts to Be Left Out: The Neurocognitive Overlap Between Physical and Social Pain. In *Sydney Symposium of Social Psychology Series. The social outcast: Ostracism, social exclusion, rejection, and bullying*.

Nakata, H., Sakamoto, K., & Kakigi, R. (2014). Meditation reduces pain-related neural activity in the anterior cingulate cortex, insula, secondary somatosensory cortex, and thalamus. *Frontiers in psychology, 5*, 1489.

Meerwijk, E., Ford, J., & J Weiss, S. (2012). Brain regions associated with psychological pain: Implications for a neural network and its relationship to physical pain. In *Brain imaging and behavior* (Vol. 7).

Simons, L. E., Pielech, M., Erpelding, N., Linnman, C., Moulton, E., Sava, S., Borsook, D. (2014). The responsive amygdala: treatment-induced alterations in functional connectivity in pediatric complex regional pain syndrome. *Pain, 155* (9), 1727–1742.

Kropf, E., Syan, S. K., Minuzzi, L., & Frey, B. N. (2018). From anatomy to function: the role of the somatosensory cortex in emotional regulation. *Revista Brasileira de Psiquiatria (Sao Paulo, Brazil: 1999)*, 0.

Etkin, A., Egner, T., & Kalisch, R. (2011). Emotional processing in anterior cingulate and medial prefrontal cortex. *Trends in Cognitive Sciences, 15* (2), 85–93.

Melzack, R., & Wall, P. D. (1962). On the nature of cutaneous sensory mechanisms. *Brain: A Journal of Neurology, 85*, 331–356.

Melzack, R., & Wall, P. D. (1965). Pain mechanisms: a new theory. *Science (New York, N.Y.), 150* (3699), 971–979.

Kandel, E., Mack, S., Kandel, E. R., Dodd, J. S., Schwartz, J., & Jessell, T. (2000). *Principles of Neural Science, Fourth Edition*. McGraw-Hill Companies, Incorporated.

Kumar, raj, Keshri, U., & Sharma, J. (2013). FLUPIRTINE: A MINI REVIEW. *Journal of Drug Delivery and Therapeutics, 3* (6), 113-116.

Kumar, S., Gupta, R., Kaleem, A. M., & Pandey, A. (2014). Mitigation of pain and anaesthetic drugs. *OA Anaesthetics, 2* (1), 2.

Cashman, J. N. (1996). The mechanisms of action of NSAIDs in analgesia. *Drugs, 52 Suppl 5*, 13–23.

Cross, S. A. (1994). Pathophysiology of pain. *Mayo Clinic Proceedings, 69* (4), 375–383.

Willis, W. D., & Westlund, K. N. (1997). Neuroanatomy of the pain system and of the pathways that modulate pain. *Journal of Clinical Neurophysiology: Official Publication of the American Electroencephalographic Society, 14* (1), 2–31.

Herdegen, T., & Leah, J. D. (1998). Inducible and constitutive transcription factors in the mammalian nervous system: control of gene expression by Jun, Fos and Krox, and CREB/ATF proteins. *Brain Research. Brain Research Reviews, 28* (3), 370—490.

Malcangio, M., & Bowery, N. G. (1996). GABA and its receptors in the spinal cord. *Trends in Pharmacological Sciences, 17* (12), 457–462.

Yaksh, T. L. (1997). Pharmacology and mechanisms of opioid analgesic activity. *Acta Anaesthesiologica Scandinavica, 41* (1 Pt 2), 94–111.

Dickenson, A. H. (1997). NMDA receptor antagonists: interactions with opioids. *Acta Anaesthesiologica Scandinavica, 41* (1 Pt 2), 112–115.

Carpenter, M. B., & Sutin, J. (1983). *Human neuroanatomy*. Baltimore: Williams & Wilkins.

Tamam, S., & Ahmad, A. H. (2017). Love as a Modulator of Pain. *The Malaysian journal of medical sciences: MJMS, 24* (3), 5-14.

M Wozniak, K., Rojas, C., Wu, Y., & S Slusher, B. (2012). The role of glutamate signaling in pain processes and its regulation by GCP II inhibition. *Current medicinal chemistry*, *19* (9), 1323-1334.

Hamilton, S. G., & McMahon, S. B. (2000). ATP as a peripheral mediator of pain. *Journal of the Autonomic Nervous System*, *81* (1–3), 187–194.

Naser, P. V, & Kuner, R. (2018). Molecular, Cellular and Circuit Basis of Cholinergic Modulation of Pain. *Neuroscience*, *387*, 135–148.

Feng, Y.-P., Wang, J., Dong, Y.-L., Wang, Y.-Y., & Li, Y.-Q. (2015). The roles of neurotensin and its analogues in pain. *Current Pharmaceutical Design*, 21 (7), 840–848.

Argoff, C. (2011). Mechanisms of pain transmission and pharmacologic management. *Current Medical Research and Opinion*, *27* (10), 2019–2031.

Shenoy, S. S., & Lui, F. (2018). Biochemistry, Endogenous Opioids. In *StatPearls [Internet]*. StatPearls Publishing.

Enna, S. J., & McCarson, K. E. (2006). The role of GABA in the mediation and perception of pain. *Advances in pharmacology*, *54*, 1-27.

Urch C. (2007). Normal Pain Transmission. *Reviews in pain, 1* (1), 2–6.

Woll, P. J. (1991). Neuropeptide growth factors and cancer. *British journal of cancer*, 63 (3), 469.

Schou, W. S., Ashina, S., Amin, F. M., Goadsby, P. J., & Ashina, M. (2017). Calcitonin gene-related peptide and pain: a systematic review. *The journal of headache and pain*, *18* (1), 34.

LaPelusa, A., & Jan, A. (2019). *Biochemistry, Bombesin*. Treasure Island (FL).

Ashina, M., Bendtsen, L., Jensen, R., Ekman, R., & Olesen, J. (1999). Plasma levels of substance P, neuropeptide Y and vasoactive intestinal polypeptide in patients with chronic tension-type headache. *Pain, 83* (3), 541–547.

Brain, S. D., & Cox, H. M. (2006). Neuropeptides and their receptors: innovative science providing novel therapeutic targets. *British journal of pharmacology*, *147 Suppl 1* (Suppl 1), S202–S211.

Husband, T. (2016). *The chemistry of human nature*. Cambridge: Royal Society of Chemistry.

Perception & Modality

Weor, S. A. (2012). *The Perfect Matrimony: The Door to Enter Into Initiation: Why Sex and Religion are Inseparable*. Brooklyn, N.Y: Glorian Publishing.

Wisdoms Friend. (n.d). Death and Darkness, Life and Light: The Separation. *Christian-Faith*. Retrieved from https://www.christian-faith.com/death-and-darkness-life-and-light-the-separation/

Greene, L., & Hand, R. (2011). *Saturn: A new look at an old devil*. San Francisco, Calif: Weiser Books.

Macey, S. L. (2013). *Encyclopedia of Time. In Garland Reference Library of Social Science*. New York: Routledge.

Pike, A. (1871). *Morals and Dogma of the Ancient and Accepted Scottish Rite of Freemasonry*. Mansfield Centre, CT: Martino Pub.

Abel, E. L. (2009). *Death Gods: An Encyclopedia of the Rulers, Evil Spirits, and Geographies of the Dead*. Westport, Conn: Greenwood Press.

Tamam, S., & Ahmad, A. H. (2017). Love as a Modulator of Pain. *The Malaysian journal of medical sciences: MJMS, 24* (3), 5–14.

Russell, W. (1974). *The Universal One*. Swannanoa, Waynesboro, Virginia: University of Science and Philosophy.

Eisenberger, N. I., & Lieberman, M. D. (2005). Why It Hurts to Be Left Out: The Neurocognitive Overlap Between Physical and Social Pain. In *Sydney Symposium of Social Psychology Series. The social outcast: Ostracism, social exclusion, rejection, and bullying*.

McMillan, D. W. (2013). *Emotion Rituals: A resource for therapists and clients*. New York: Routledge.

Eisigner, R. M. (2000). Questioning cynicism. *Society, 37* (5), 55.

Mustain, M. (2014). *Overcoming cynicism: William James and the metaphysics of engagement*. New York: Bloomsbury.

Paloş, R., & Vîşcu, L. (2014). Anxiety, automatic negative thoughts, and unconditional self-acceptance in rheumatoid arthritis: a preliminary study. *ISRN rheumatology, 2014*, 317259.

Cacioppo, J. T., & Hawkley, L. C. (2009). Perceived social isolation and cognition. *Trends in cognitive sciences, 13* (10), 447–454.

Sturgeon, J. A., & Zautra, A. J. (2016). Social pain and physical pain: shared paths to resilience. *Pain management, 6* (1), 63-74.

Tuan, Y.-F. (1998). *Escapism*. Baltimore, Md: Johns Hopkins University Press.

Abe, M., & Heine, S. (1995). *Buddhism and interfaith dialogue*. Honolulu: University of Hawaii Press.

Chapter 10

Sadness

McMillan, D. W. (2013). *Emotion Rituals: A resource for therapists and clients*. New York: Routledge.

Fink, G. (2016). *Stress: Concepts, Cognition, Emotion, and Behavior: Handbook of Stress Series*. San Diego, CA: Academic Press.

Selye, H. (1985). History and present status of the stress concept. *In* A. Monat & R.S. Lazarus, eds. *Stress and Coping*, 2nd ed. New York: Columbia University.

Selye, H. (1956). *The Stress of Life*. New York: McGraw-Hill.

Selye, H. (1976). *Stress in health and disease*. Reading, MA: Butterworth.

Selye, H. (1982). History and present status of the stress concept. *In* L. Goldberger and S. Breznitz (Eds). *Handbook of stress: Theoretical and clinical aspects*. New York: The Free Press.

Selye, H. (1975). Confusion and controversy in the stress field. *Journal of Human Stress*, 1 (2), 37–44.

Parrott, W. G. (2001). *Emotions in social psychology: Essential readings*. Philadelphia, PA: Psychology Press.

Puglisi-Allegra, S., & Andolina, D. (2015). Serotonin and stress coping. *Behavioural Brain Research, 277*, 58–67.

McMillan, D. W. (2013). *Emotion Rituals: A resource for therapists and clients*. New York: Routledge.

Vingerhoets, A. J. J. M. (2013). *Why only humans weep: Unravelling the mysteries of tears*. Oxford: Oxford University Press.

Nestler, E. J., Hyman, S. E., & Malenka, R. C. (2008). *Molecular Neuropharmacology: A Foundation for Clinical Neuroscience, Second Edition*. McGraw Hill Professional.

Langley, L. (2011). *Crazy little thing: How love and sex drive us mad*. Berkeley, Calif: Viva Editions.

Watanabe, M., Maemura, K., Kanbara, K., Tamayama, T., & Hayasaki, H. (2002). GABA and GABA receptors in the central nervous system and other organs. *International Review of Cytology, 213*, 1–47.

Freed, P. J., & Mann, J. J. (2007). Sadness and Loss: Toward a Neurobiopsychosocial Model. *American Journal of Psychiatry, 164* (1), 28–34.

Vingerhoets, A. (2013). *Why Only Humans Weep: Unravelling the Mysteries of Tears*. Oxford: Oxford University Press.

Coon, D., & Mitterer, J. O. (2015). Introduction to Psychology: Gateways to Mind and Behavior. *Cengage Learning*.

McDougall, P., Hymel, S., Vaillancourt, T., & Mercer, L. (2001). The consequences of childhood peer rejection. *Interpersonal rejection*, 213-247.

Leary, M. R., & Downs, D. L. (1995). *Interpersonal Functions of the Self-Esteem Motive*. In M. H. Kernis (Ed.), Efficacy, Agency, and Self-Esteem. pp. 123–144. Boston, MA: Springer US.

Goleman, D. (1995). *Emotional Intelligence*. London: Bantam Books.

Leary M. R. (2015). Emotional responses to interpersonal rejection. *Dialogues in clinical neuroscience*, 17 (4), 435–441.

Sperling, M. B., & Berman, W. H. (1994). *Attachment in Adults: Clinical and Developmental Perspectives*. Guilford Press.

Ohmae, S. (2012). [The difference between depression and melancholia: two distinct conditions that were combined into a single category in DSM-III]. *Seishin shinkeigaku zasshi = Psychiatria et neurologia Japonica, 114* (8), 886–905.

Scott, W. D., Ingram, R. E., & Shadel, W. G. (2003). Hostile and sad moods in dysphoria: Evidence for cognitive specificity in attributions. *Journal of Social and Clinical Psychology, 22* (3), 233-252.

Ekstrand, D. W. (2018, September 25). *THE FOUR HUMAN TEMPERAMENTS*. Retrieved from http://www. thetransformedsoul.com/additional-studies/miscellaneous-studies/the-four-human-temperaments.

Childs, G. (1995). *Understand your temperament*. London: Sophia.

Eysenck, H. J. (1967). *The biological basis of personality*. Springfield, Ill: C.C. Thomas.

Neurochemistry & Physiology

McMillan, D. W. (2013). *Emotion Rituals: A resource for therapists and clients*. New York: Routledge.

Freed, P. J., & Mann, J. J. (2007). Sadness and Loss: Toward a Neurobiopsychosocial Model. *American Journal of Psychiatry, 164* (1), 28–34.

Vingerhoets A. J. J. M, Cornelius R. R., Van Heck G. L., Becht M. C. (2000). Adult crying: a model and review of the literature. *Rev. Gen. Psychol.* (4) 354–377.

Hofer, M. A. (1984). Relationships as regulators: a psychobiologic perspective on bereavement. *Psychosomatic Medicine, 46* (3), 183–197.

Hofer, M. A. (1994). Early relationships as regulators of infant physiology and behavior. *Acta Paediatrica (Oslo, Norway: 1992). Supplement, 397*, 9–18.

Berridge, K. C., & Robinson, T. E. (2003). Parsing reward. *Trends in Neurosciences, 26* (9), 507–513.

Uvnas-Moberg, K. (1998). Oxytocin may mediate the benefits of positive social interaction and emotions. *Psychoneuroendocrinology, 23* (8), 819–835.

Bartels, A., & Zeki, S. (2004). The neural correlates of maternal and romantic love. *NeuroImage, 21* (3), 1155–1166.

Zubieta, J.-K., Ketter, T. A., Bueller, J. A., Xu, Y., Kilbourn, M. R., Young, E. A., & Koeppe, R. A. (2003). Regulation of human affective responses by anterior cingulate and limbic mu-opioid neurotransmission. *Archives of General Psychiatry, 60* (11), 1145–1153.

Schirmer, A. (2014). *Emotion*. Thousand Oaks, CA: SAGE Publications.

Turner, R. A., Altemus, M., Enos, T., Cooper, B., & McGuinness, T. (1999). Preliminary research on plasma oxytocin in normal cycling women: investigating emotion and interpersonal distress. *Psychiatry, 62* (2), 97–113.

Liebowitz, M. R. (1984). *The Chemistry of Love*. New York: Berkley Books.

Fisher, H. (1994). The nature of romantic love. *Journal of NIH Research, 6* (4).

Patil, Y. (2014). The Chemistry of Love. *International Journal of Scientific & Engineering Research, 5* (4), 1317-1319.

Chaudhry, S. R., & Bhimji, S. S. (2018). Biochemistry, Endorphin. In *StatPearls [Internet]*. StatPearls Publishing.

Amir, S., Brown, Z. W., & Amit, Z. (1980). The role of endorphins in stress: Evidence and speculations. *Neuroscience & Biobehavioral Reviews, 4* (1), 77–86.

Khajehei, M., & Behroozpour, E. (2018). Endorphins, oxytocin, sexuality and romantic relationships. *World J Obstet Gynecol, 7* (2), 17-23.

Emmelkamp, P. M. G. (1989). *Anxiety Disorders: A Practitioner's Guide*. John Wiley and Sons.

Panksepp, J. (1998). *Series in affective science. Affective neuroscience: The foundations of human and animal emotions.* New York, NY, US: Oxford University Press.

Eapen, V., Dadds, M., Barnett, B., Kohlhoff, J., Khan, F., Radom, N., & Silove, D. M. (2014). Separation anxiety, attachment and inter-personal representations: disentangling the role of oxytocin in the perinatal period. *PloS one, 9* (9), e107745.

Knoll, A. T., & Carlezon, W. A., Jr (2010). Dynorphin, stress, and depression. *Brain research, 1314*, 56–73.

DeHaven, R. N., Mansson, E., Daubert, J. D., & Cassel, J. A. (2005). Pharmacological characterization of human kappa/mu opioid receptor chimeras that retain high affinity for dynorphin A. *Current Topics in Medicinal Chemistry, 5* (3), 303–313.

Lutz, P. E., & Kieffer, B. L. (2013). Opioid receptors: distinct roles in mood disorders. *Trends in neurosciences, 36* (3), 195–206.

Watanabe, H., Fitting, S., Hussain, M. Z., Kononenko, O., Iatsyshyna, A., Yoshitake, T., … Bakalkin, G. (2015). Asymmetry of the endogenous opioid system in the human anterior cingulate: a putative molecular basis for lateralization of emotions and pain. *Cerebral cortex* (New York, N.Y.: 1991), 25 (1), 97–108.

Clavin, W. (2002, April 15). Brain opiate may explain why some people are less susceptible to addiction. *Nature's own antidote to cocaine*. Retrieved from https://www.dynorphin. com.

Bruchas, M. R., Land, B. B., & Chavkin, C. (2010). The dynorphin/kappa opioid system as a modulator of stress-induced and pro-addictive behaviors. *Brain research, 1314*, 44–55. Schwarzer C. (2009). 30 years of dynorphins--new insights on their functions in neuropsychiatric diseases. *Pharmacology & therapeutics, 123* (3), 353–370.

Przewlocki, R., Lason, W., Konecka, A. M., Gramsch, C., Herz, A., & Reid, L. D. (1983). The opioid peptide dynorphin, circadian rhythms, and starvation. *Science (New York, N.Y.), 219* (4580), 71–73.

Chavkin, C., & Koob, G. F. (2016). Dynorphin, Dysphoria, and Dependence: the Stress of Addiction. *Neuropsychopharmacology: official publication of the American College of Neuropsychopharmacology, 41* (1), 373–374.

Weaver, J. (2011). Crying Women Turn Men Off. *Scientific American Mind, 22* (2), 6-6.

Gračanin, A., Bylsma, L. M., & Vingerhoets, A. J. (2014). Is crying a self-soothing behavior?. *Frontiers in psychology,* 5, 502.

Frey II, W. H., Desota-Johnson, D., Hoffman, C., & McCall, J. T. (1981). Effect of stimulus on the chemical composition of human tears. *American journal of ophthalmology, 92* (4), 559-567.

Walter, C. (2006). Why Do We Cry? *Scientific American Mind,* 17 (6), 44-51.

Hall, D. (2012). *Mind - Body - God Connection.* eBookIt.com.

Vingerhoets, A. (2013). *Why Only Humans Weep: Unravelling the Mysteries of Tears.* Oxford: Oxford University Press.

Dell'Amore, C. (2011, January 8) Women's Tears Reduce Sex Drive in Men, Study Hints. *National Geographic.* Retrieved from https://news.nationalgeographic .com /news /2011 /01/110106-womens-tears-sex-drive-turn-off-sexual-health-arousal-men-science/

Gračanin, A., van Assen, M. A. L. M., Omrčen, V., Koraj, I., & Vingerhoets, A. J. J. M. (2017). Chemosignalling effects of human tears revisited: Does exposure to female tears decrease males' perception of female sexual attractiveness? *Cognition and Emotion,* 31 (1), 139–150.

Freed, P. J., & Mann, J. J. (2007). Sadness and Loss: Toward a Neurobiopsychosocial Model. *American Journal of Psychiatry, 164* (1), 28–34.

Peyron, R., Laurent, B., & Garcia-Larrea, L. (2000). Functional imaging of brain responses to pain. A review and meta-analysis (2000). *Neurophysiologie Clinique = Clinical Neurophysiology, 30* (5), 263–288.

Denton, D., Shade, R., Zamarippa, F., Egan, G., Blair-West, J., McKinley, M, Fox, P. (1999). Neuroimaging of genesis and satiation of thirst and an interoceptor-driven theory of origins of primary consciousness. *Proceedings of the National Academy of Sciences of the United States of America, 96* (9), 5304–5309.

Liotti, M., Brannan, S., Egan, G., Shade, R., Madden, L., Abplanalp, B, Denton, D. (2001). Brain responses associated with consciousness of breathlessness (air hunger). *Proceedings of the National Academy of Sciences of the United States of America, 98* (4), 2035–2040.

Athwal, B. S., Berkley, K. J., Hussain, I., Brennan, A., Craggs, M., Sakakibara, R, Fowler, C. J. (2001). Brain responses to changes in bladder volume and urge to void in healthy men. *Brain: A Journal of Neurology, 124* (Pt 2), 369–377.

Levesque, J., Joanette, Y., Mensour, B., Beaudoin, G., Leroux, J.-M., Bourgouin, P., & Beauregard, M. (2003). Neural correlates of sad feelings in healthy girls. *Neuroscience*, *121* (3), 545–551.

Levesque, J., Eugene, F., Joanette, Y., Paquette, V., Mensour, B., Beaudoin, G, Beauregard, M. (2003). Neural circuitry underlying voluntary suppression of sadness. *Biological Psychiatry*, *53* (6), 502–510.

Lane, R. D., & Nadel, L. (2002). *Cognitive Neuroscience of Emotion*. Oxford University Press.

Parvizi, J., Anderson, S. W., Martin, C. O., Damasio, H., & Damasio, A. R. (2001). Pathological laughter and crying: a link to the cerebellum. *Brain : A Journal of Neurology*, *124* (Pt 9), 1708–1719.

Brody, A. L., Barsom, M. W., Bota, R. G., & Saxena, S. (2001). Prefrontal-subcortical and limbic circuit mediation of major depressive disorder. *Seminars in Clinical Neuropsychiatry*, *6* (2), 102–112.

Perception & Modality

Freed, P. J., & Mann, J. J. (2007). Sadness and Loss: Toward a Neurobiopsychosocial Model. *American Journal of Psychiatry*, *164* (1), 28–34.

Scherer, K. R. (2005). Appraisal Theory. In *Handbook of Cognition and Emotion*. John Wiley & Sons, Ltd.

Kazdin, A. E. (2000). *Encyclopedia of Psychology*. American Psychological Association.

Dalgleish, T., & Power, M. (2000). *Handbook of Cognition and Emotion*. John Wiley & Sons.

Mann, J. J. (1988). *Phenomenology of Depressive Illness*. New York: Human Sciences Press.

Yuen, K. S. L., & Lee, T. M. C. (2003). Could mood state affect risk-taking decisions? *Journal of Affective Disorders*, *75* (1), 11–18.

Storbeck, J., & Clore, G. L. (2005). With sadness comes accuracy; with happiness, false memory: mood and the false memory effect. *Psychological Science*, *16* (10), 785–791.

Bodenhausen, G. V, Gabriel, S., & Lineberger, M. (2000). Sadness and susceptibility to judgmental bias: the case of anchoring. *Psychological Science*, *11* (4), 320–323.

McMillan, D. W. (2013). *Emotion Rituals: A resource for therapists and clients*. New York: Routledge.

Droit-Volet, S., Fayolle, S., & Gil, S. (2011). Emotion and Time Perception: Effects of Film-Induced Mood. *Frontiers in Integrative Neuroscience*, 5, 33.

Gil, S., & Droit-Volet, S. (2009). Time perception, depression and sadness. *Behavioural processes*, *80* (2), 169-176.

Contrada, R., & Baum, A. (2010). *The Handbook of Stress Science: Biology, Psychology, and Health*. New York: Springer Publishing Company.

Amir, S., Brown, Z. W., & Amit, Z. (1980). The role of endorphins in stress: Evidence and speculations. *Neuroscience & Biobehavioral Reviews, 4* (1), 77–86.

Chapter 11

Happiness

Ricard, M. (2011). *The art of happiness: A guide to developing life's most important skill.* London: Atlantic.

Algoe, S. B., & Haidt, J. (2009). Witnessing excellence in action: the 'other-praising' emotions of elevation, gratitude, and admiration. *The Journal of Positive Psychology, 4* (2), 105–127.

Graham, M. C., Priddy, L., & Graham, S. (2014). *Facts of Life: Ten Issues of Contentment.* Denver, Colorado: Outskirts Press.

McMillan, D. W. (2013). *Emotion Rituals: A resource for therapists and clients.* New York: Routledge**.**

Franken, R. E. (1994). *Human motivation.* Pacific Grove, Calif: Brooks/Cole Pub. Co.

Maslow, A. H. (1943). A theory of human motivation. *Psychological Review, 50* (4), 370–396.

Maslow, A., & Lewis, K. J. (1987). Maslow's hierarchy of needs. *Salenger Incorporated, 14,* 987.

McSweeney, F. K., & Murphy, E. S. (2014). *The Wiley-Blackwell handbook of operant and classical conditioning.* Hoboken, NJ: Wiley-Blackwell.

Martinich, A. P., & Hobbes, T. (1998). *A Hobbes dictionary.* Malden, Mass: Blackwell.

Gere, C. (2017). *Pain, pleasure, and the greater good: From the Panopticon to the Skinner box and beyond.* Chicago, Illinois; London, England: The University of Chicago Press.

Fredrickson, B. L. (2001). The role of positive emotions in positive psychology. The broaden-and-build theory of positive emotions. *The American psychologist,* 56 (3), 218–226.

Tamam, S., & Ahmad, A. H. (2017). Love as a Modulator of Pain. *The Malaysian journal of medical sciences: MJMS, 24* (3), 5–14.

Freed, P. J., & Mann, J. J. (2007). Sadness and Loss: Toward a Neurobiopsychosocial Model. *American Journal of Psychiatry, 164* (1), 28–34.

Samardzic, J., Jadzic, D., Hencic, B., Jancic, J., & Strac, D. S. (2018). Introductory Chapter: GABA/Glutamate Balance: A Key for Normal Brain Functioning. GABA And Glutamate: *New Developments In Neurotransmission Research,* 1.

Lydiard, R. B. (2003). The role of GABA in anxiety disorders. *The Journal of clinical psychiatry, 64,* 21-27.

Abdou, A. M., Higashiguchi, S., Horie, K., Kim, M., Hatta, H., & Yokogoshi, H. (2006). Relaxation and immunity enhancement effects of γ-Aminobutyric acid (GABA) administration in humans. *Biofactors*, *26* (3), 201-208.

Dfarhud, D., Malmir, M., & Khanahmadi, M. (2014). Happiness & Health: The Biological Factors- Systematic Review Article. *Iranian journal of public health, 43* (11), 1468-77.

Neurochemistry & Physiology

Kop, W. J., Synowski, S. J., Newell, M. E., Schmidt, L. A., Waldstein, S. R., & Fox, N. A. (2011). Autonomic nervous system reactivity to positive and negative mood induction: the role of acute psychological responses and frontal electrocortical activity. *Biological psychology*, 86 (3), 230–238.

May, R. (1999). *Freedom and Destiny*. W. W. Norton & Company.

Goleman, D. (1995). *Emotional Intelligence*. London: Bantam Books.

McMillan, D. W. (2013). *Emotion Rituals: A resource for therapists and clients*. New York: Routledge.

Lane, R. D. (2000). Neural correlates of conscious emotional experience. *Cognitive neuroscience of emotion*, 345-370.

Foster, A. E., & Yaseen, Z. S. (2019). *Teaching Empathy in Healthcare: Building a New Core Competency*. Switzerland: Springer Nature.

Human Physiology. (1967). *In Biovue Modern Biology Series*. Burlington, MA: Jones & Bartlett Publishers.

Perry, E. K. (2010). New Horizons in the Neuroscience of Consciousness. *In Advances in Consciousness Research*. Philadelphia: John Benjamins Publishing.

Dfarhud, D., Malmir, M., & Khanahmadi, M. (2014). Happiness & Health: The Biological Factors- Systematic Review Article. *Iranian journal of public health, 43* (11), 1468-77.

Abdou, A. M., Higashiguchi, S., Horie, K., Kim, M., Hatta, H., & Yokogoshi, H. (2006). Relaxation and immunity enhancement effects of γ-Aminobutyric acid (GABA) administration in humans. *Biofactors*, *26* (3), 201-208.

Edwards, G., & Babor, T. F. (2012). *Addiction and the Making of Professional Careers*. New Brunswick: Transaction Publishers.

Hill, M. N., & Patel, S. (2013). Translational evidence for the involvement of the endocannabinoid system in stress-related psychiatric illnesses. *Biology of mood & anxiety disorders*, *3* (1), 19.

Minkov, M., & Bond, M. H. (2017). A genetic component to national differences in happiness. *Journal of Happiness Studies*, *18* (2), 321-340.

Potter, P. M. (2007). *Growing Beyond Our Genetics: Adolescence and Beyond*. Lulu.com.

Franken, R.E. (1994). *Human Motivation*, 3rd ed. Belmont, CA: Brooks/Cole Publishing Company.

Rokade, P. B. (2011). Release of endomorphin hormone and its effects on our body and moods: A review. In *International Conference on Chemical, Biological and Environment Sciences*. pp. 436-438.

Freed, P. J., & Mann, J. J. (2007). Sadness and Loss: Toward a Neurobiopsychosocial Model. *American Journal of Psychiatry, 164* (1), 28–34.

DeHaven, R. N., Mansson, E., Daubert, J. D., & Cassel, J. A. (2005). Pharmacological characterization of human kappa/mu opioid receptor chimeras that retain high affinity for dynorphin A. *Current Topics in Medicinal Chemistry, 5* (3), 303–313.

Dfarhud, D., Malmir, M., & Khanahmadi, M. (2014). Happiness & Health: The Biological Factors- Systematic Review Article. *Iranian journal of public health, 43* (11), 1468-77.

Watanabe, H., Fitting, S., Hussain, M. Z., Kononenko, O., Iatsyshyna, A., Yoshitake, T., Bakalkin, G. (2015). Asymmetry of the endogenous opioid system in the human anterior cingulate: a putative molecular basis for lateralization of emotions and pain. *Cerebral cortex (New York, N.Y: 1991), 25* (1), 97–108.

Jain, R. (2020). *The science and practice of wellness: Interventions for happiness, enthusiasm, resilience, and optimism (HERO)*. New York: W.W. Norton & Company,

Tantimonaco, M., Ceci, R., Sabatini, S., Catani, M. V., Rossi, A., Gasperi, V., & Maccarrone, M. (2014). Physical activity and the endocannabinoid system: an overview. *Cellular and Molecular Life Sciences*: CMLS, 71 (14), 2681–2698.

Fitzgerald, P. J. (2013). Elevated Norepinephrine may be a Unifying Etiological Factor in the Abuse of a Broad Range of Substances: Alcohol, Nicotine, Marijuana, Heroin, Cocaine, and Caffeine. Substance Abuse: *Research and Treatment, 7*.

Robinson, J. D. (2001). *Mechanisms of Synaptic Transmission: Bridging the Gaps (1890-1990)*. Oxford: Oxford University Press.

Kringelbach, M. L., & Berridge, K. C. (2010). The functional neuroanatomy of pleasure and happiness. *Discovery medicine*, 9 (49), 579-87.

Davidson, R. J. (2001). Toward a biology of personality and emotion. *ANNALS-NEW YORK ACADEMY OF SCIENCES, 935*, 191-207.

Davidson, R. J., & Lutz, A. (2008). Buddha's Brain: Neuroplasticity and Meditation. *IEEE signal processing magazine*, 25 (1), 176–174.

Desmond, T. (2016). *Self-compassion in psychotherapy: Mindfulness-based practices for healing and transformation*. New York: W.W. Norton & Company

Wilson, C. R. E., Gaffan, D., Browning, P. G. F., & Baxter, M. G. (2010). Functional localization within the prefrontal cortex: missing the forest for the trees? *Trends in Neurosciences*, 33 (12), 533–540.

Davidson, R.J. (2003). Affective neuroscience and psychophysiology: toward a synthesis. *Psychophysiology, 40 5*, 655-65.

Urry, H. L., Nitschke, J. B., Dolski, I., Jackson, D. C., Dalton, K. M., Mueller, C. J., … Davidson, R. J. (2004). Making a Life Worth Living: Neural Correlates of Well-Being. *Psychological Science,* 15 (6), 367–372.

Lutz, A., Greischar, L. L., Rawlings, N. B., Ricard, M., & Davidson, R. J. (2004). Long-term meditators self-induce high-amplitude gamma synchrony during mental practice. *Proceedings of the National Academy of Sciences of the United States of America, 101* (46), 16369–16373.

van Dijk, A., Klompmakers, A. A., Feenstra, M. G. P., & Denys, D. (2012). Deep brain stimulation of the accumbens increases dopamine, serotonin, and noradrenaline in the prefrontal cortex. *Journal of Neurochemistry*, 123 (6), 897–903.

Del Arco, A., & Mora, F. (2008). Prefrontal cortex-nucleus accumbens interaction: in vivo modulation by dopamine and glutamate in the prefrontal cortex. *Pharmacology, Biochemistry, and Behavior,* 90 (2), 226–235.

Boecker, H., Sprenger, T., Spilker, M. E., Henriksen, G., Koppenhoefer, M., Wagner, K. J., & Tolle, T. R. (2008). The runner's high: opioidergic mechanisms in the human brain. *Cerebral cortex, 18* (11), 2523-2531.

Sprouse-Blum, A. S., Smith, G., Sugai, D., & Parsa, F. D. (2010). Understanding endorphins and their importance in pain management. *Hawaii medical journal, 69* (3), 70–71.

Perception & Modality

Freed, P. J., & Mann, J. J. (2007). Sadness and Loss: Toward a Neurobiopsychosocial Model. *American Journal of Psychiatry*, 164 (1), 28–34.

McMillan, D. W. (2013). *Emotion Rituals: A resource for therapists and clients.* New York: Routledge.

Fisher, H. (2000). Lust, attraction, attachment: Biology and evolution of the three primary emotion systems for mating, reproduction, and parenting. *Journal of Sex Education and Therapy, 25* (1), 96-104.

Fisher, H. E., Aron, A., Mashek, D., Li, H., & Brown, L. L. (2002). Defining the brain systems of lust, romantic attraction, and attachment. *Archives of sexual behavior, 31* (5), 413-419.

Fisher, H. E. (1992). *Anatomy of love: A natural history of mating, marriage, and why we stray.* New York: Fawcett Columbine.

Fairbairn, C. E., Briley, D. A., Kang, D., Fraley, R. C., Hankin, B. L., & Ariss, T. (2018). A meta-analysis of longitudinal associations between substance use and interpersonal attachment security. *Psychological bulletin, 144* (5), 532–555.

Dfarhud, D., Malmir, M., & Khanahmadi, M. (2014). Happiness & Health: The Biological Factors- Systematic Review Article. *Iranian journal of public health, 43* (11), 1468-77.

Tamam, S., & Ahmad, A. H. (2017). Love as a Modulator of Pain. *The Malaysian journal of medical sciences: MJMS, 24* (3), 5–14.

Lazarus, R.S., & Folkman, S. (1984). *Stress, Appraisal and Coping.* New York: Springer.

Lazarus, R.S., & Launier, R. (1978). Stress-related transactions between person and environment. *In* L. A. Pervin & M. Lewis, eds. *Perspectives in Interactional Psychology.* New York: Plenum.

Georgiadis, J. R., & Kringelbach, M. L. (2012). The human sexual response cycle: brain imaging evidence linking sex to other pleasures. *Progress in Neurobiology, 98* (1), 49–81.

Kruger, T. H. C., Hartmann, U., & Schedlowski, M. (2005). Prolactinergic and dopaminergic mechanisms underlying sexual arousal and orgasm in humans. *World Journal of Urology*, 23 (2), 130–138.

Siegel, S., & Allan, L. G. (1998). Learning and homeostasis: drug addiction and the McCollough effect. *Psychological Bulletin, 124* (2), 230–239.

Magon, N., & Kalra, S. (2011). The orgasmic history of oxytocin: Love, lust, and labor. *Indian journal of endocrinology and metabolism, 15 Suppl 3* (Suppl3), S156–S161.

Sunderwirth, S., Milkman, H., & Jenks, N. (1996). Neurochemistry and sexual addiction. *Sexual Addiction & Compulsivity, 3* (1), 22–32.

Lee, N. M., Carter, A., Owen, N., & Hall, W. D. (2012). The neurobiology of overeating. Treating overweight individuals should make use of neuroscience research, but not at the expense of population approaches to diet and lifestyle. *EMBO reports*, 13 (9), 785–790.

Anselme, P., & Robinson, M. J. (2013). What motivates gambling behavior? Insight into dopamine's role. *Frontiers in behavioral neuroscience*, 7, 182.

Kovacs, G. L., Sarnyai, Z., & Szabo, G. (1998). Oxytocin and addiction: a review. *Psychoneuroendocrinology, 23* (8), 945–962.

Olsen, C. M. (2011). Natural rewards, neuroplasticity, and non-drug addictions. *Neuropharmacology*, 61 (7), 1109–1122.

Kim, A., & Maglio, S. J. (2018). Vanishing time in the pursuit of happiness. *Psychonomic Bulletin & Review, 25* (4), 1337–1342.

Simen, P., & Matell, M. (2016). Why does time seem to fly when we're having fun? *Science (New York, N.Y.), 354* (6317), 1231–1232.

Burdick, A. (2018). *Why time flies: A mostly scientific investigation*. New York: Simon & Schuster.

Coull, J. T., Cheng, R. K., & Meck, W. H. (2011). Neuroanatomical and neurochemical substrates of timing. *Neuropsychopharmacology*, 36 (1), 3-25.

Lyman, S. M. (1989). *The seven deadly sins: Society and evil*. Dix Hills, N.Y: General Hall.

In Syrjälä, H., & In Leipämaa-Leskinen, H. (2018). *Seven deadly sins in consumption*. Northampton, MA: Edward Elgar Pub, Inc.

Russell, W. (1974). *The Universal One*. Swannanoa, Waynesboro, Virginia: University of Science and Philosophy.

Chapter 12

Enlightenment

Fine Dictionary. (n.d.). *Enlightenment*. Retrieved February, 08,2020. Retrieved from http://www.Finedictionary.com/enlightenment.html

Dove, F. (2021, February 24). CONSCIOUSNESS, *What Is In The Word "Enlightenment"?* Retrieved fromhttps://freedomdove.net/2021/02/24/what-is-in-the-word-enlightenment/

Harvey, P. (2012). *An Introduction to Buddhism: Teachings, History and Practices*. Cambridge: Cambridge University Press.

Erricker, C., Lowndes, J., & Bellchambers, E. (2010). *Primary Religious Education - A New Approach: Conceptual Enquiry in Primary RE*. New York: Routledge.

Lyman, S. M. (1989). *The seven deadly sins: Society and evil*. Dix Hills, N.Y: General Hall.

In Syrjälä, H., & In Leipämaa-Leskinen, H. (2018). *Seven deadly sins in consumption*. Northampton, MA: Edward Elgar Pub, Inc.

Wilson, E. (2012). *Emotions and Spirituality in Religions and Spiritual Movements*. Lanham, Md: University Press of America.

"When the even was come, they brought unto him many that were possessed with devils: and he cast out the spirits with his word, and healed all that were sick." (Matthew 6:18, King James Version).

Tsering, T., Zopa, T., & McDougall, G. (2006). *Buddhist Psychology: The Foundation of Buddhist Thought*. In *Buddhism Series*. Simon and Schuster.

Carrette, J. R., & King, R. (2005). *Selling spirituality: The silent takeover of religion*. London: Routledge.

Kapleau, R. P. (2013). *The Three Pillars of Zen*. Knopf Doubleday Publishing Group.

Giletto, J. B. (2017). *Mystical Memories*. Outskirts Press.

The Ultimate Goal of Life MEN- Moksha Enlightenment Nirvana: The A to Z of Spirituality. (2019). Bangalore: AiR Institute of Realization.

Sayadaw, W., de Silva, L., Nyanasobhano, B., Karunaratna, S., Bullis, D., van Loon, L., others. (2012). *Collected Bodhi Leaves Volume V: Numbers 122 to 157*.Shri Lanka: Buddhist Publication Society.

Carter, R. E., & Yuasa, Y. (2012). *Encounter with Enlightenment: A Study of Japanese Ethics*. Albany, NY: State University of New York Press.

Harvey, P. (2012). *An Introduction to Buddhism: Teachings, History and Practices.* Cambridge: Cambridge University Press.

Wikipedians, B. (n.d.). *Religion.* PediaPress.

Leeming, D. A. (1998). *Mythology: The Voyage of the Hero.* Oxford: Oxford University Press.

Saurer, M. M. (2005). *A Comparison of World Religions: Ancient to Modern-Day.* Xlibris US.

Mahan, A., & Friedrich, R. (2003). *A Critical History of Philosophy.* Xulon Press.

Braun, R. L. (2000). *Jesus: His Name and Titles: A Devotional and Theological Study.* Lincoln, NE: iUniverse.

Buswell, R. E. (2004). *Encyclopedia of Buddhism.* New York: Macmillan Reference USA/Thomson/Gale.

Zanzig, T. (1999). *Jesus of History, Christ of Faith.* Saint Mary's Press.

Carey, G. W., & Perry, I. E. (1920). *God-man: The Word Made Flesh.* Los Angeles: Chemistry of life Company.

Raza, S. A. (n.d.). *Law of God.* Syed Ali Raza.

Franco, R. (2013). *Comparative etymological Dictionary of classical Indo-European languages: Indo-European - Sanskrit - Greek - Latin.* Charleston, S.C: Createspace Independent Pub.

S, Acharya. (2004). *Suns of God: Krishna, Buddha and Christ Unveiled.* Kempton, Illinois: Adventures Unlimited Press.

Hall, M. P. (2018). *The Occult Anatomy of Man.* Chicago: Muriwai Books.

Initiates, T. (1908). *The Kybalion: A Study of the Hermetic Philosophy of Ancient Egypt and Greece.* Chicago, Illinois: The Yogi Publication Society.

Wasserstrom, S. M. (1999). *Religion after Religion: Gershom Scholem, Mircea Eliade, and Henry Corbin at Eranos.* Princeton: Princeton University Press.

Jung, C., Shamdasani, S., & Hull, R. (1969). *Four Archetypes: (From Vol. 9, Part 1 of the Collected Works of C. G. Jung).* PRINCETON; OXFORD: Princeton University Press.

Tharpa, T. (2018). Tibetan Buddhist Essentials: A Study Guide for the 21st Century: Volume 1: Introduction, Origin, and Adaptation. *In Tibetan Buddhist Essentials.* Bylakuppe, India: Sera Jey Monastic University.

Gilchrist, C. (2015). *Alchemy - the great work: A brief history of Western hermeticism.* London: Coronet.

Christopher, L. T. (2006). *Kabbalah, magic, and the great work of self-transformation: A complete course.* Woodbury, Minn: Llewellyn Publications.

Adams, D. J. (2019). *Enlightenment and Illumination: Spiritual Wisdom from Djwahl Khul*. Bloomington, IN: AuthorHouse.

Chandran, R., & Pollock, R. M. (2019). *33 Keys to Ascension: A Comprehensive Guide for Ascension & Enlightenment for the Modern-Day World*. Flagstaff, AZ: Light Technology Publishing.

Stone, J. D., & White, S. M. (2001). *The Ascension Names and Terms Glossary*. Lincoln, NE: iUniverse.

Virtue, D. (2004). *Archangels & Ascended Masters*. Carlsbad, Calif. Hay House.

Levi, E., & Waite, A. E. (1968). *Transcendental Magic*. Weiser Books.

Einspahr, J. (2010). The Beginning that Never Was: Mediation and Freedom in Rousseau's Political Thought. *The Review of Politics,* 72 (3), 437-461.

Burgoyne, T. H. (1999). *The Light of Egypt: Volume One, the Science of the Soul and the Stars*. Denver, Colorado: Book Tree.

Yukteswar, S. (2011). *The holy science: Kaivalya darsanam*. Los Angeles, Calif: Self-Realization Fellowship.

Weor, S. A. (2012). *The Perfect Matrimony: The Door to Enter Into Initiation: Why Sex and Religion are Inseparable.* Brooklyn, N.Y: Glorian Publishing.

Kaplan, A. G., & Sedney, M. A. (1980). *Psychology and sex roles: an androgynous perspective*. Boston: Little, Brown and Company.

Goddard, D. (1999). *The Tower of Alchemy: An Advanced Guide to the Great Work.* York Beach, ME: Red Wheel Weiser.

"There is neither Jew nor Greek, there is neither bond nor free, there is neither male nor female: for ye are all one in Christ Jesus." (Galatians 3:28, King James Version).

"So God created man in his own image, in the image of God created he him; male and female created he them." (Genesis 1:27, King James Version).

Neurochemistry & Physiology

Carey, G. W., & Perry, I. E. (1920). *God-man: The Word Made Flesh*. Los Angeles: Chemistry of life Company.

Kerr, K. M., & Francis, J. R. (2019). *The God Design: Secrets of the Mind, Body and Soul*. Seek Vision.

Braun, R. L. (2000). *Jesus: His Name and Titles: A Devotional and Theological Study.* Lincoln, NE: iUniverse.

Liddell, H. G., Scott, R., Jones, H. S., & McKenzie, R. (1958). *A Greek-English lexicon compiled by Henry George Liddell,..and Robert Scott,... New ed. rev. and augm. throughout by... Henry Stuart Jones*. Oxford: Clarendon.

Britannica, T. Editors of Encyclopaedia (2021, March 31). *Golgotha*. *Encyclopedia Britannica*. Retrieved from https://www.britannica.com/place/Golgotha

"This mystery has been kept in the dark for a long time, but now it's out in the open. God wanted everyone, not just Jews, to know this rich and glorious secret inside and out, regardless of their background, regardless of their religious standing. The mystery in a nutshell is just this: Christ is in you, so therefore you can look forward to sharing in God's glory. It's that simple." (Colossians 1, 26:29, The Message (MSG)).

"If the LORD delights in us, he will bring us into this land and give it to us, a land that flows with milk and honey." (Numbers 14:8, English Standard Version 2016).

Baribeau, D. A., & Anagnostou, E. (2015). Oxytocin and vasopressin: linking pituitary neuropeptides and their receptors to social neurocircuits. *Frontiers in neuroscience*, *9*, 335.

Sacral vertebrae. (n.d.) *Collins English Dictionary – Complete and Unabridged, 12th Edition 2014*. (1991, 1994, 1998, 2000, 2003, 2006, 2007, 2009, 2011, 2014). Retrieved February 8 2022 from https://www.thefreedictionary.com/Sacral+vertebrae

"I am the living bread that came down from heaven. If anyone eats of this bread, he will live forever. And the bread that I will give for the life of the world is my flesh." (John 6:51, English Standard Version).

Nandi, I. (2019). Christ-Mary-Energy: Self-Empowerment, Initiations, Practice. Germany: BoD - Books on Demand.

"Early the next morning Jacob took the stone he had placed under his head and set it up as a pillar and poured oil on top of it." (Genesis 28:18)

"So Jacob named the place Peniel, for he said, "I have seen God face to face, yet my life has been preserved." (Genesis 32:30, New American Standard Bible)

Langley, L. (2011). *Crazy little thing: How love and sex drive us mad*. Berkeley, Calif: Viva Editions.

Georgiadis, J. R., & Kringelbach, M. L. (2012). The human sexual response cycle: brain imaging evidence linking sex to other pleasures. *Progress in Neurobiology*, 98 (1), 49–81.

Fisher, H. E., Aron, A., Mashek, D., Li, H., & Brown, L. L. (2002). Defining the brain systems of lust, romantic attraction, and attachment. *Archives of sexual behavior*, *31* (5), 413-419.

Newell, R., & Gournay, K. (2008). *Mental Health Nursing E-Book: An Evidence Based Approach*. London: Elsevier Health Sciences.

Tariri, B. (2013). *Desexed*. Boomington, IN: Author House.

Love, T., Laier, C., Brand, M., Hatch, L., & Hajela, R. (2015). Neuroscience of Internet Pornography Addiction: A Review and Update. *Behavioral sciences (Basel, Switzerland)*, 5 (3), 388-433.

Craig, A. D. (2009). How do you feel - now? The anterior insula and human awareness. *Nature Reviews Neuroscience*, *10*, 59.

Decety, J., & Jackson, P. L. (2004). The Functional Architecture of Human Empathy. *Behavioral and Cognitive Neuroscience Reviews, 3* (2), 71–100.

Jackson, P. L., Brunet, E., Meltzoff, A. N., & Decety, J. (2006). Empathy examined through the neural mechanisms involved in imagining how I feel versus how you feel pain. *Neuropsychologia, 44* (5), 752–761.

Karnath, H.-O., Baier, B., & Nägele, T. (2005). Awareness of the Functioning of One's Own Limbs Mediated by the Insular Cortex? *Journal of Neuroscience, 25* (31), 7134–7138.

Farrer, C., & Frith, C. D. (2002). Experiencing Oneself vs Another Person as Being the Cause of an Action: The Neural Correlates of the Experience of Agency. *NeuroImage, 15* (3), 596–603.

Tsakiris, M., Hesse, M. D., Boy, C., Haggard, P., & Fink, G. R. (2006). Neural Signatures of Body Ownership: A Sensory Network for Bodily Self-Consciousness. *Cerebral Cortex, 17* (10), 2235–2244.

Phan, K. L., Wager, T., Taylor, S. F., & Liberzon, I. (2002). Functional neuroanatomy of emotion: a meta-analysis of emotion activation studies in PET and fMRI. *NeuroImage, 16* (2), 331–348.

Gianaros, P. J., Derbyshire, S. W., May, J. C., Siegle, G. J., Gamalo, M. A., & Jennings, J. R. (2005). Anterior cingulate activity correlates with blood pressure during stress. *Psychophysiology, 42* (6), 627–635.

Luu, P., & Posner, M. I. (2003). Anterior cingulate cortex regulation of sympathetic activity. *Brain,* 126 (10), 2119–2120.

Sevinc, G., Gurvit, H., & Spreng, R. N. (2017). Salience network engagement with the detection of morally laden information. *Social Cognitive and Affective Neuroscience, 12* (7), 1118–1127.

Strigo, I. A., & Craig, A. D. (2016). Interoception, homeostatic emotions and sympathovagal balance. *Philosophical transactions of the Royal Society of London. Series B, Biological sciences, 371* (1708), 20160010.

Tahmasian, M., Rochhausen, L., Maier, F., Williamson, K. L., Drzezga, A., Timmermann, L., Eggers, C. (2015). Impulsivity is Associated with Increased Metabolism in the Fronto-Insular Network in Parkinson's Disease. *Frontiers in behavioral neuroscience, 9,* 317.

Bush, G., Vogt, B. A., Holmes, J., Dale, A. M., Greve, D., Jenike, M. A., & Rosen, B. R. (2002). Dorsal anterior cingulate cortex: A role in reward-based decision making. *Proceedings of the National Academy of Sciences, 99* (1), 523–528.

Oppenheimer, S. M., Gelb, A., Girvin, J. P., & Hachinski, V. C. (1992). Cardiovascular effects of human insular cortex stimulation. *Neurology, 42* (9), 1727–1732.

Perception & Modality

Kruger, T. H. C., Hartmann, U., & Schedlowski, M. (2005). Prolactinergic and dopaminergic mechanisms underlying sexual arousal and orgasm in humans. *World Journal of Urology*, 23 (2), 130–138.

Ben-Jonathan, N., & Hnasko, R. (2001). Dopamine as a prolactin (PRL) inhibitor. *Endocrine Reviews*, 22 (6), 724–763.

Carmichael, M. S., Humbert, R., Dixen, J., Palmisano, G., Greenleaf, W., & Davidson, J. M. (1987). Plasma oxytocin increases in the human sexual response. *The Journal of Clinical Endocrinology and Metabolism*, 64 (1), 27–31.

Hull, E. M., Muschamp, J. W., & Sato, S. (2004). Dopamine and serotonin: influences on male sexual behavior. *Physiology & Behavior*, 83 (2), 291–307.

Will, R. G., Hull, E. M., & Dominguez, J. M. (2014). Influences of dopamine and glutamate in the medial preoptic area on male sexual behavior. *Pharmacology, Biochemistry, and Behavior*, *121*, 115–123.

Carey, G. W., & Perry, I. E. (1920). *God-man: The Word Made Flesh*. Los Angeles: Chemistry of life Company.

"There is neither Jew nor Greek, there is neither bond nor free, there is neither male nor female: for ye are all one in Christ Jesus." (Galatians 3:28, King James Version).

"So God created man in his own image, in the image of God created he him; male and female created he them." (Genesis 1:27, King James Version).

Love, T., Laier, C., Brand, M., Hatch, L., & Hajela, R. (2015). Neuroscience of Internet Pornography Addiction: A Review and Update. *Behavioral sciences (Basel, Switzerland)*, 5 (3), 388-433.

Kirby, E. W., Carson, C. C., & Coward, R. M. (2015). Tramadol for the management of premature ejaculation: a timely systematic review. *International Journal Of Impotence Research*, 27, 121.

Sastry, B. V, Janson, V. E., & Owens, L. K. (1991). Significance of substance P- and enkephalin-peptide systems in the male genital tract. *Annals of the New York Academy of Sciences*, *632*, 339–353.

Bancroft, J. (2005). The endocrinology of sexual arousal, *Journal of Endocrinology*, *186* (3), 411-427.

Bodri, W. (2001). *Socrates and the Enlightenment Path*. Boston, MA: Red Wheel Weiser.

Lloyd, J. W. (1931). *The Karezza Method Or Magnetation: The Art of Connubial Love*. Privately printed for the author.

Langley, L. (2011). *Crazy little thing: How love and sex drive us mad*. Berkeley, Calif: Viva Editions.

Georgiadis, J. R., & Kringelbach, M. L. (2012). The human sexual response cycle: brain imaging evidence linking sex to other pleasures. *Progress in Neurobiology*, 98 (1), 49–81.

Fisher, H. E., Aron, A., Mashek, D., Li, H., & Brown, L. L. (2002). Defining the brain systems of lust, romantic attraction, and attachment. *Archives of sexual behavior, 31* (5), 413-419.

Newell, R., & Gournay, K. (2008). *Mental Health Nursing E-Book: An Evidence Based Approach*. London: Elsevier Health Sciences.

Tariri, B. (2013). *Desexed.* Boomington, IN: Author House.

Love, T., Laier, C., Brand, M., Hatch, L., & Hajela, R. (2015). Neuroscience of Internet Pornography Addiction: A Review and Update. *Behavioral sciences (Basel, Switzerland)*, 5 (3), 388-433.

Graham, D. N. (2010). *The 80/10/10 diet: Balancing your health, your weight, and your life one luscious bite at a time*. Key Largo, Fla: FoodnSport Press.

Ehret, A. (2015). *Mucusless Diet Healing System: A Scientific Method of Eating Your Way to Health*. ReadHowYouWant.com.

Moss, M. (2013). *Salt, Sugar, Fat: How the Food Giants Hooked Us.* New York: Random House.

Campbell, T. C., & Campbell, T. M. (2016). *The China Study: Revised and Expanded Edition: The Most Comprehensive Study of Nutrition Ever Conducted and the Startling Implications for Diet, Weight Loss, and Long-Term Health*. Dallas, Texas: BenBella Books, Inc.

Campbell, J. (2008). *The Hero with a Thousand Faces*. In *Bollingen Series*. New World Library.

Campbell, J., Epstein, E. L., & Foundation, J. C. (2003). *Mythic Worlds, Modern Words: On the Art of James Joyce*. In *Collected Works of Joseph Campbell*. Novato, CA: New World Library.

Buswell, R. E., & Lopez, D. S. (2013). *The Princeton Dictionary of Buddhism*. Princeton University Press.

Robison, A. J., & Nestler, E. J. (2011). Transcriptional and epigenetic mechanisms of addiction. *Nature reviews. Neuroscience*, 12 (11), 623-37.

Renthal, W., & Nestler, E. J. (2008). Epigenetic mechanisms in drug addiction. *Trends in molecular medicine, 14* (8), 341–350.

D'Adamo, A. (2015). *Science Without Bounds: A Synthesis of Science, Religion and Mysticism*. CreateSpace Independent Publishing Platform.

Nitrogeno 02: *International review of Operative Alchemy. (2016). In Nitrogeno - International Review of Operative Alchemy*. Fontana Editore.

Final Word

"Words kill, words give life; they're either poison or fruit - you choose." - Proverbs 18:21 (MSG)

"In the beginning was the Word, and the Word was with God, and the Word was God." - John 1:1 (NIV)